Reflections on motivation

Other titles in the series

Reflections on Citizenship in a multilingual world
Ed. Kim Brown and Margot Brown
REFLECTIONS ON PRACTICE 8

Reflections on ICT
Ed. Terry Atkinson
REFLECTIONS ON PRACTICE 7

Reflections on grammar-implicit language teaching
Margaret Wells
REFLECTIONS ON PRACTICE 5

Reflections on the target language
Peter S Neil
REFLECTIONS ON PRACTICE 4

Reflections on Modern Languages in primary education: six UK case studies
Ed. Alison Hurrell and Peter Satchwell
REFLECTIONS ON PRACTICE 3

Reflections on reading: from GCSE to A level
Ed. Mike Grenfell
REFLECTIONS ON PRACTICE 2

Series editor: Mike Calvert

Reflections on motivation

Edited by Gary Chambers

The views expressed in this book are those of the editor and contributors and do not necessarily reflect the views of CILT.

First published 2001
by the Centre for Information on Language Teaching and Research (CILT)
20 Bedfordbury, London WC2N 4LB

ISBN 1 902031 44 X

2005 2004 2003 2002 2001 / 10 9 8 7 6 5 4 3 2 1

A catalogue record for this book is available from the British Library

Printed in Great Britain by Copyprint UK Ltd

CILT Publications are available from: **Central Books,** 99 Wallis Rd, London E9 5LN. Tel: 0845 458 9910. Fax: 0845 458 9912. Book trade representation (UK and Ireland): **Broadcast Book Services,** Charter House, 27a London Road, Croydon CR0 2RE. Tel: 020 8681 8949. Fax: 020 8688 0615.

Contents

Introduction

Gary Chambers

What do I do with those pupils with no interest in languages who are only in the classroom because they have to be?

This was a question asked recently by a teacher attending a Goethe Institut in-service seminar in the North-East of England. It was the only question the seminar leader could not answer. Had he known the answer he would have bottled it, sold it and retired by the end of the month.

In the end, it is a question of motivation. How easily that last word rolls off the tongue. It ought to be a much longer word and much more difficult to pronounce given its complexity and the challenges it presents. Have a look at one of those in-flight magazines you find in the seat pocket on a plane. Open it at the page giving details of all the international flights in and out of Heathrow. What a tangled mess this seems to be. There are strands criss-crossing the entire world. They are all interlinked. It is hard to conceive of such an enormous and complicated network actually functioning. In spite of the complexity, they all converge on Heathrow. If motivation could be viewed under a microscope, I suspect it would look rather like that: a mass of strands interlinking to determine an individual's behaviour.

When teachers of modern languages consider a pupil's motivation to learn French/German/Spanish, it is not only the complexity of motivation they have to grapple with but also the complexity of modern languages. Dörnyei (1994: 274) describes a language as i) a communication coding system, ii) an integral part of an individual's identity and iii) the most important channel of social organisation embedded in the culture of the community where it is used. This takes the learning of a new language beyond vocabulary lists, verb tables and grammar, and into the realms of the environment, society and the make-up of the individual. So who ever claimed that teaching languages was simple?

As the title of this book suggests, *Reflections on Motivation* provides rather more than a set of handy hints for the fraught teacher of languages to implement with the disaffected Year 9 on a Tuesday afternoon. The remainder of this introductory chapter takes the form of a review of the current state of play *vis à vis* motivation and foreign language learning. This is then followed by a series of contributions reflecting a mixture of research and classroom experience. Yes, the reader is provided with insights into activities which worked. Much more important, however, are the reasons **why** they worked. The reader is provided with a rationale and in some cases a theoretical underpinning to the success of the activities. It is this marrying of theory and practice which may provide the template for the development of other successful activities in different contexts.

What is motivation?

What is this motivation upon which we are reflecting? It is far from easy to come up with a satisfactory definition. Any definition is likely to be contested and/or used in an inconsistent manner where its meaning differs to suit differing contexts. Users of the term may be quite clear as to what motivation means for their own purposes. Unless this understanding is well-founded, legitimate and shared, however, confusion and obfuscation can result. A definition based on an unclear understanding of what motivation is only serves to deepen the confusion.

So what makes it so difficult? After all, motivation is only the driving force that makes us do the things we do. Have you given any thought to the multiplicity of interlinking factors which may contribute to that driving force? We may be conscious of some of these factors. There may be others about which we are blissfully unaware. Motivation is so multifaceted that it is almost impossible to articulate a definition which covers all facets satisfactorily and with any conciseness. This has not prevented many academics from trying:

Instinct theory (nineteenth century): Freud maintained that human behaviour was motivated by a) the life instinct (*Eros*), the basis for sexual motivation, and b) the death instinct (*Thanatos*), which underlay aggression. Freud regarded these instincts as part of the individual's unconscious. William James took the functionalist view: an individual's instincts, such as fear, sociability, cleanliness and love, focused on the central instinct to survive.

Drive theory (early twentieth century; see Cannon, 1932): a drive may motivate not a single behaviour but various behaviours based on the same need. Hunger, for example, may motivate not only eating but also restlessness before mealtimes. Eating then reduces the drive.

Neobehaviourism (Hull, 1943): this proposed that the probability of a given behaviour was based on three factors: a) drive determined by need; b) incentive – the perceived capacity of the external stimulus to reduce the need; c) habit – the extent of the individual's experience in performing the behaviour.

Behaviourism (Skinner, 1957): this focuses on stimulus-response associations and cause rather than need and reason for action. Skinner's experiments on rats led to the development of definitions for reinforcement (any operation that increases the rate of response), punishment (any operation which decreases the rate of response), shaping (the step by step procedure in training an animal by positive reinforcement of each phase of the desired behaviour) and schedules of reinforcement (i.e. only certain responses are reinforced).

Cognitive approach (Weiner, 1972; Jung, 1978): unlike behaviourism, which focuses on the observable, this approach focuses on that which cannot be observed; it postulates that action can only be understood in relation to cognitive factors, e.g. thought processes, intentions, expectations, interpretations of given situations. Weiner's (1980) 'attributions', for example, are causal explanations for a certain behaviour. Four common attributions for success are ability, effort, luck and task difficulty. Ability and effort are internal to the subject and are therefore her/his responsibility. Luck and task difficulty are external and the subject has no influence over these. Subjects who are normally successful tend to attribute success to effort and ability. If unsuccessful, they blame effort, with the implication that this internal trait can be modified. Subjects who are normally unsuccessful and experience success, tend to attribute this success to external factors such as luck or level of task difficulty ('It was easy, Miss'). Any failure is attributed to lack of ability.

Each of these theories makes an important contribution to the attempt to establish the nature of motivation but, taken in isolation, proves unsatisfactory. An eclectic approach may get closer to the ideal. It cannot be ignored, however, that different motives may lie behind the same action i) for different people or ii) for the same person on different occasions. An individual may have multiple motives for a particular action. To positively identify someone's motivation, therefore, is a considerable challenge.

Perhaps Dörnyei and Ottó (1998: 65) get closest to a definition which acknowledges most appropriately the multidimensional and ever changing nature of motivation:

> *The dynamically changing cumulative arousal in a person that initiates, directs, coordinates, amplifies, terminates, and evaluates the cognitive and motor processes whereby initial wishes and desires are selected, prioritised, operationalised and (successfully or unsuccessfully) acted out.*

Motivation, school and modern languages

So we may now have some idea of what makes us do the things we do generally but what about the school context and the modern language teaching and learning context in particular?

The work of Gardner and his associates is well known in the field of motivation and second foreign language learning. Gardner's **socio-educational model** has been the subject of researchers' interest since its development in the mid-eighties and only in the nineties has it been viewed with a more critical eye (see Dörnyei, 1994). It is summarised below primarily because of the insight it gives into the work that has informed its creation.

Gardner (1985: 124–145) describes how the socio-educational model is soundly based on seven other foreign language learning models each of which can be placed into one of two categories:

1. those with a focus on **linguistic process** – i.e. which address individual differences in second language achievement. To this category belong the following models:

   (i) **Monitor model** (Krashen, 1978, 81,82): there are two language systems, one conscious (attention to form rather than content), the other subconscious (focus on the message rather than grammatical accuracy).

   (ii) **Conscious re-inforcement model** (Carroll, 1981): language learning begins when the individual has the intent to communicate: depending on the intent, knowledge and context, the individual responds; if the response achieves the desired goal, it is reinforced; this may result in the response being repeated in similar contexts and the acquisition of knowledge about the nature of the language itself.

   (iii) **Strategy model** (Bialystok, 1978): the model has three levels or stages:

   (a) input – exposure to the language;

   (b) knowledge – conscious and intuitive knowledge about the language;

   (c) output – response (spontaneous or requiring deliberation).

   To these levels are applied four types of strategies:

   (a) formal practising – focus on grammar, pronunciation, linguistic patterns;

   (b) functional practising – e.g. communication with speakers of the target language; watching films in the target language;

   (c) monitoring – modifying language behaviour based on knowledge of the code;

   (d) inferencing – e.g. inferring the meaning of a previously unknown word based on the context in which it is located.

2. those with a **social process** focus – i.e. attention to the social, psychological variables which facilitate or impede second language acquisition. To this category belong the following models:

(iv) **Social psychological model of second language acquisition** (Lambert, 1963a, 1963b, 1967, 1974): students learning a second language *must be both able and willing to adopt various aspects of behaviour, including verbal behaviour, which characterise members of the other linguistic-cultural group* (1967: 102). The model focuses on affective factors such as ethnocentric tendencies, attitudes towards the other community, orientation towards language learning and motivation.

(v) **Acculturation model** (Schumann, 1978a, 1978b): like Lambert, Schumann assumes the importance of identification with the target language community but identifies other factors including social, affective, personality, cognitive, biological, aptitude, personal and instructional.

(vi) **Social context model** (Clément, 1980): this places emphasis on the cultural milieu of the language communities involved. Central to the model is the quality of motivation in the learner which may emanate at the extremes from a social context where a) there is little contact with the target language community, learning of the target language is not encouraged at school or at home and fear of assimilation with the target language community may be strong and b) where first and second languages have equal status, contact between the two communities is close, there is considerable support from school and home and a high degree of integrativeness.

(vii) **Intergroup model** (Giles and Byrne, 1982): this focuses on the second language acquisition of a linguistic minority group and stresses the importance of maintenance of a positive self-concept. Those who fear assimilation and tend not to be successful in second language acquisition are likely to avoid contact with speakers of the target language (the linguistic majority group) and concentrate on formal learning contexts, e.g. school. Those who are integratively orientated tend to be more successful in acquiring the second language and actively seek contact with the target language community in informal contexts.

Gardner's **socio-educational model** focuses on four classes of variable:

1. **Social milieu:** the influence of the cultural context in which the second language acquisition takes place. If the cultural belief is that to learn a foreign language is difficult, then the general level of achievement is likely to be low (self-fulfilling prophecy). The converse is also true.

2. **Individual differences:** focus on four types of individual differences which influence achievement directly: a) intelligence (speed of learning); b) language aptitude (cognitive and verbal abilities); c) motivation (effort and desire); d) situational anxiety (inhibitions).

3. **Language acquisition contexts:** a) formal contexts – language classroom or any situation in which the individual receives training, explanations or drills;

b) informal contexts – situations where instruction is not the primary aim, e.g. listening to the radio, watching television, conversation.

4. **Learning outcomes:** a) linguistic outcomes – proficiency in the language/ grammar/vocabulary/pronunciation/fluency, etc; b) non-linguistic outcomes – the attitudes and values which derive from the experience.

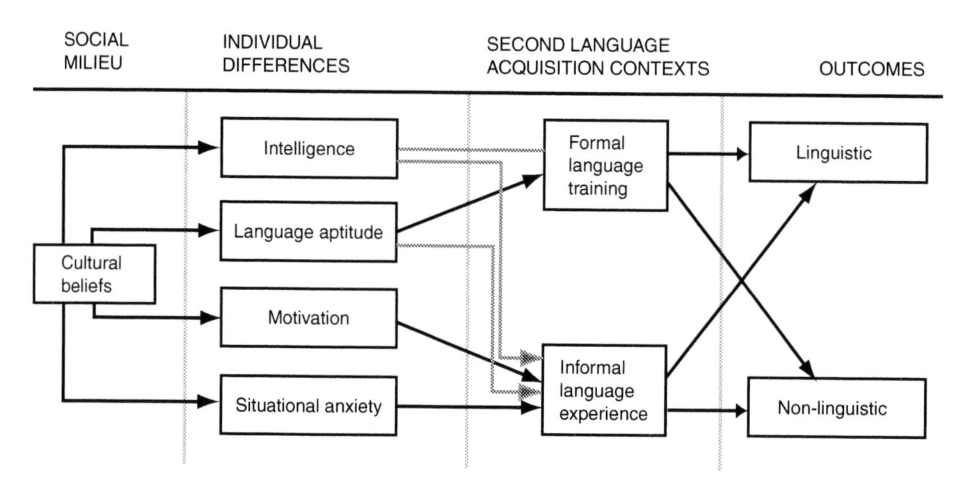

Figure 1.1 – Gardner's socio-educational model

The work of Gardner has much to offer the teacher of foreign and second languages in the UK context. Some circumspection and criticality are appropriate, however. Although Gardner claims to place under scrutiny '*the context of the student acquiring a second language in the school setting, often in environments where immediate access to the second language community is limited, if not virtually non-existent*' (1985: 4), his research often has a context where foreign language learners have, if not immediate, then near access to the target language community, e.g. learning French in Canada. The learners, their families and friends may have a view of the target language community based on considerable experience of living with or close to that community. They may leave the formal learning context of the classroom and move easily into an informal learning context where they hear and see the target language in authentic situations. This is unlikely to be the case for the foreign language learner in the UK for whom, with few exceptions, the informal learning context is not so accessible. Opinions on the target language community may be based on holidays, articles in newspapers and magazines, television programmes and/or hearsay.

So what are the challenges posed by the classroom context? Are the pupils in the class because they want to be or because they have to be? (Gardner's **cultural beliefs** and **situational anxiety**.) How much choice do they have in what they are learning in the foreign language class? (**Motivation**.) How confident do they feel about what they are doing? (**Social milieu** and **individual differences.**) Do they feel that there is a reasonable chance of being successful in what they are doing or are they laden with the failure of past learning experience? (**Individual differences** and **non linguistic outcomes.**) How do they perceive the teacher? Helpful and approachable? Obstructive and scary? How do they perceive the language learning experience? Pleasant? Dull? (**Situational anxiety.**) Do they see the point in foreign language learning? Have they had much contact with target language speakers? Do they perceive any likelihood of contact with them? (**Social milieu** and **informal language experience.**) Are they afraid of what their peers might think as they endeavour to speak in this strange code? (**Situational anxiety.**) What perceptions of foreign language learning do they bring from their homes? (**Social milieu.**)

Dörnyei's motivational framework

The above questions are some of those which challenge teachers of foreign languages on a daily basis. Critics of Gardner argue that his approach does not provide the answer.

> *While acknowledging unanimously the fundamental importance of the Gardnerian socio-educational model, researchers were also calling for a more pragmatic, education-centred approach to motivation research, which would be consistent with the perceptions of practising teachers and which would also be in line with the current results of mainstream educational psychological research.* (Dörnyei 1994: 273)

Dörnyei (*op. cit.*: 280–282) offers a framework and a list of recommendations which may help provide positive answers. It should be recognised that this framework has been developed in a TEFL/TESOL context and so may have elements not immediately transferable to the secondary school modern languages context. The framework has three levels: **language level; learner level; learning situation level.**

Language level – this relates to motivational factors such as the cultural dimension, perceptions of the target language community, the potential usefulness of competence in the target language.

- Include a sociocultural component – video; music; target language (TL) visitors. Develop learners' cross-cultural awareness systematically – focus on similarities as well as differences.
- Promote student contact with TL speakers – exchanges; penfriends; class-links. Develop learners' instrumental motivation – discuss role of the TL in the world, its usefulness to the pupils and to the community.

Learner level – this relates to the learner's self-appraisal of strengths and weaknesses and how this appraisal affects their learning; this may include factors such as anxiety, perceived target language competence, perceptions of past experiences, self-esteem.

- Develop students' self-confidence – role of praise; encouragement; reinforcement; success.
- Promote students' self-efficacy with regard to achieving learning goals – teach them learning and communication strategies; information processing and problem-solving strategies; help them develop realistic expectations.
- Promote favourable self-perceptions of competence in TL – focus on what they can do rather than on what they cannot do; mistakes are not bad; they are a necessary part of learning.
- Decrease student anxiety – create a supportive, accepting, non-punitive learning environment.
- Promote motivation-enhancing attributions – help students see the link between effort and outcome; help them see real reasons for past failure, e.g. lack of effort, failure to understand instructions, implementation of inappropriate strategies, rather than lack of ability.
- Encourage students to set attainable sub-goals, e.g. to learn five new words each day; may be part of personalised learning plan.

Learning situation level – this consists of three aspects:

(i) **Course-specific motivational components** – this relates to the motivational influence of the syllabus, teaching materials, teaching methods, learning activities.

  - The syllabus should be relevant.
  - Course content should be attractive – authentic, accessible materials; varied media.
  - Discuss choice of teaching materials with the students – identifying their strengths and weaknesses.
  - Arouse and sustain curiosity and attention – introduce the unexpected; break up routine; change seating; make students move around the room from time to time.
  - Increase students' interest and involvement in the tasks – challenge; games; puzzles; competitions; pair- and group-work.
  - Match difficulty of tasks with students' abilities.

- Increase student expectancy of task-fulfilment – appropriate preparation for the task; transparency of assessment methods and marking criteria.
- Facilitate student satisfaction – wall-displays of work; presentations; celebrations of success.

(ii) **Teacher-specific motivational components** – this relates to the teacher-pupil relationship, the teacher's approach to behaviour management, the promotion of 'sharing' of ideas and views between pupils as well as teacher and pupils, the provision of motivating feedback.

- Try to be empathetic, congruent and accepting.
- Be a 'facilitator' rather than a 'drill sergeant'.
- Promote learner autonomy – provide real choices; share responsibility.
- Model student interest in TL learning – share how the TL and its learning enrich your life; show your enthusiasm and commitment.
- Introduce tasks in such a way as to stimulate intrinsic motivation and help internalise extrinsic motivation – present them as learning opportunities to be valued rather than imposed demands to be resisted; point out the interesting; the exotic; stress the usefulness.
- Use motivating feedback – make it positive and informative; do not overreact to errors.

(iii) **Group-specific motivational components** – the promotion of collaboration; shared goals; shared norms of behaviour.

- Increase the group's goal-orientedness – encourage discussion of group's goals and extent to which they are being achieved.
- Promote internalisation of classroom norms – negotiate with students and agree modes of behaviour which are acceptable and best promote learning.
- Help maintain internalised classroom norms – adhere to them yourself and don't ignore any violations.
- Minimise the detrimental effect of evaluation on intrinsic motivation – encourage each student to be the best that she or he can be; avoid comparison with other students; make evaluations private rather than public; seek student's opinion.
- Promote development of group cohesion and enhance intermember relations – create situations in which students can get to know each other – group activities; outings; exchanges.
- Use co-operative learning techniques – group-work; include evaluation of group's rather than individuals' performance.

The motivational context

If we are to understand the challenge which motivation in the modern languages classroom poses, and come to grips with possible strategies for meeting that challenge, it is important to gain some appreciation of the initiatives and innovations of the time, the beginnings of the twenty-first century. What, then, is the motivational context within which the teaching and learning of modern foreign languages in the UK is taking place?

Why bother with foreign languages?

How many times have you been asked this question by a disaffected Year 9 or Year 10 pupil. '*Everybody speaks English*', is the core of the pupil's argument. Were this the view of an adult, we would probably, in most cases, regard ourselves in a very strong position to counter it. However, to provide a rationale which a pubescent teenager can understand, appreciate and willingly accept, is a real challenge. Wrestling with this problem may drive some colleagues to believe that the pupil may well be right and that for some teenagers learning foreign languages is of dubious value. We may find it hard to convince our pupils of the point of foreign language learning but Jones (1998: 6) provides us with one reason (of many) which may provide comfort and motivation for the teacher, if not the learner:

> *And if we are to be effective communicators, we need an appreciation of cultural differences: language learning is the privileged route to understanding this and to beginning to acquire such an appreciation.*

When other nationalities have to speak in English, it is important that native speakers of English appreciate the constraints this imposes. Learning a foreign language gives access to this appreciation. This justifies the learning of a foreign language by those who (claim they) will never venture into a country where English is not spoken. Hagen (1998: 17) provides useful statistics and interesting examples for the frustrated teacher of languages to underpin the argument that monolingualism is unlikely to serve the native speaker of English adequately:

- *just over one in five exporters (21%) claim to face (or have faced) a language barrier;*
- *just under one in five (19%) face (or have faced) a cultural barrier (principally in Japan, Mid-East, China, France, Germany and Italy);*
- *22% of exporters report an increased need for language skills;*
- *nearly one in seven (14%) had found that using British English posed a communication barrier for foreign speakers of the language. Companies had apparently failed to understand the distinction between British*

> *English and the use of international or mid-Atlantic English, its abbreviated, simplified cousin.*

Hagen suggests that having English as a mother-tongue can be a double-edged sword: it is the most widely used business language in the world (and gives British business a head start if they use it appropriately), but it also lulls people into believing that it suffices for all occasions throughout the world.

When considering reasons for learning languages, many pupils who see beyond the obligation to do so imposed by the National Curriculum, identify their usefulness for career purposes (Lee et al, 1998: 44) and therefore may be seduced by Hagen's evidence. As the authors of *The invisible child* (Lee *et al,* 1998) point out, however, a focus on the utilitarian value of languages to the exclusion or neglect of the cultural and social advantages, is unlikely to sustain motivation throughout the statutory period of learning (and beyond).

Most European countries (apart from the Republic of Ireland) have stolen a march on the UK (see Jones 1998: 12). English as a foreign language is treated as a 'basic skill'. Foreign language learning (usually English) is not uncommon in primary schools; in secondary schools pupils learn at least one foreign language (most commonly English) and often more, until reaching the school leaving age. (See Jones 1998: 9.) If we are not to be left (even further) behind, then the recommendations included in the Council of Europe's *Strategies in language learning and use* (Holec *et al,* 1996: 5) to promote plurilingualism should be adopted. Jones (*op.cit.*: 8) attaches to the 'socio-cultural competence' of the foreign language learner expectations embedded in reality:

A learner developing 'socio-cultural competence' may show some of the following:

- attitudes and values – an effective capacity to relinquish enthnocentric attitudes towards others, and a cognitive ability to build a relationship between different cultures;
- ability to learn – an ability to develop an interpretative system with which to gain insight into new cultural meanings, beliefs and practices;
- 'knowing-how' – the capacity to integrate attitudes and values, ability to learn and acquire knowledge in specific situations of bicultural contact;
- knowledge – the system which structures knowledge acquired.

Is there a tendency to neglect some of these factors? Is this the result of a restrictive National Curriculum, a limited, transactional syllabus and an obsession with examination performance and the related league table position?

The National Curriculum and its implications for motivation

The National Curriculum is now established as an inescapable and unavoidable feature on the modern foreign languages landscape. Like most things in life, it is something of a 'curate's egg'. It gave modern languages their proper place as a foundation subject area and, in the early days at least, promoted diversification. It has failed, however, to provide pupils with a learning experience which interests and excites them adequately to persuade them into taking a foreign language at A level.

> *Post-16 is becoming a crisis phase for MFL. At this point nine out of ten young people discontinue study of a language ... this represents a serious missed opportunity for young people.* (Boaks, 1998: 40)

While most other A level subjects have seen an increase in recruitment, the numbers taking foreign languages are in decline. (This situation is replicated in Scotland where it is reported that over the past twenty years the number of S5 students sitting Higher Grade examinations in modern languages has almost halved. (See McPake *et al*, 1999: 2.)) Diversification did not really take off (Dobson,1998: 20). A packed National Curriculum-driven timetable, recruitment difficulties plus the influence of league tables and schools' obsession with good A*–C scores have resulted in dual linguists becoming a dying breed. Where are future teachers of foreign languages going to come from? They are a scarce commodity already. Schools need and demand teachers of at least two foreign languages. Teacher training institutions are struggling to recruit graduates with even one (Asher *et al,* 1999; Boaks, 1998: 35; Towell, 1998: 49).

Recruitment is only one factor which threatens the place of modern foreign languages as a foundation subject. The introduction of short courses in languages at GCSE did little to enhance their status. One could argue that this status is undermined still further by the so called '*new flexibility at Key Stage 4*' in the revised National Curriculum (DfEE and QCA, 1999):

> *From August 2000, new regulations under Section 363 will be introduced which will allow disapplication of design and technology and/or modern foreign languages for two further purposes, in addition to work-related learning. The purposes are: 1) to allow pupils making significantly less progress than their peers to study fewer national curriculum subjects in order to consolidate their learning across the curriculum; and 2) in response to their individual strengths and talents, to allow pupils to emphasise a particular curriculum area by exchanging national curriculum subjects for further courses in that curriculum area (www.qca.org.uk/changes-to-the-nc/).*

So what does this say to pupils and their teachers about the value of learning a foreign language? What are they to believe? On the one hand, the revised

National Curriculum (*op.cit.*: 14) goes to great lengths to stress the importance of modern foreign languages: appreciation of different countries, cultures, peoples and communities; seeing oneself as a citizen of the world, not just the UK; learning about other languages and about one's own language; enhancing listening, speaking, reading and writing skills; laying the foundation of future study of other languages. This is backed up by quotations from well-known figures such as Gary Lineker, John Cleese and Trevor McDonald. On the other hand, however, the message is transmitted that while foreign languages are important, they are not so important that everyone should learn them, certainly not beyond the age of 14. What are the implications of this for motivation? Is this a step back to the future, to an era where language learning is only for the 'brighter' pupils, and an elitist area of the curriculum? Gill (1999) suggests this may well be the case:

> *At last we can dump those disaffected kids and give them something 'more appropriate' to do, and at the same time we can solve the chronic shortage of language teachers by simply not having to employ so many of them. Foreign language learning will return to a nice little niche subject, to be studied only by the truly gifted linguist, and of no use to anyone in the real world.*

She also makes the point about entitlement and equality:

> *If you're a human being, you have a gift for language: it just needs to be developed. (ibid.)*

While the revised National Curriculum may give pupils the opportunity to put to one side the school-based learning of foreign languages at the end of Key Stage 3, it is heartening that it promotes its inclusion at Key Stage 2. The inclusion of a non-statutory model programme of study may help end the '*ad hocery*' which has plagued primary foreign language teaching for so long. If this is to have a positive motivational pay-off at Key Stage 3, then it is very important that lessons are learned from Burstall *et al* (1974) and the Scottish experience (*Standards and Quality in Primary and Secondary Schools 1994–98: Modern Languages*, 1999, Scottish Office Education and Industry Department). Secondary schools have to take note of the pupils' experience at primary school and build on any foundation as appropriate. Teacher competence and confidence in primary schools are also issues which will need investment of time and money.

The OFSTED dimension and motivation

Another 'curate's egg'? The negative side of OFSTED inspections is well documented. However, where the outcome of the inspection has been positive, this has invariably been accompanied by an increase in teachers' morale and motivation. This, of course, has a knock-on effect on pupils' self-esteem (given that they have played an important role in the success), the quality of their learning experience and their motivation. Another positive aspect is what OFSTED (in addition to other research e.g .Chambers, 1999; Lee *et al*, 1998; O'Reilly-Cavani, 1997) teaches us about the pupils' learning experience which can inform our future approach to teaching. Dobson (1998) provides a comprehensive and balanced synthesis of OFSTED inspections from which the following points are drawn:

- pupils make a good start in Year 7 (where the novelty of foreign language learning offers an impetus to motivation) but many make insufficient progress over KS3 and KS4;
- some pupils are provided with insufficient opportunities to respond to progressively more demanding tasks;
- some teachers have inappropriately low expectations of pupils' ability to respond, especially in AT2;
- where teachers are able to incorporate a range of media, including video, satellite television, and IT in their lessons, this normally motivates pupils and enhances their cultural awareness by providing real images in another way.

(It is interesting to identify the similarities between these observations and the **learner level** and **language level** of Dörnyei's framework.)

There is also considerable overlap between the observations made by Dobson and those which feature in the *Quality and Standards report for Scotland* (1999). Particularly disturbing, in the light of the huge investment in Scotland's primary foreign languages project (£17 million over five years), is the observation that little account is taken after transfer to secondary school of the primary school experience. The implications of this for pupils' motivation are serious. Couple this with Dobson's comment (1998: 5) that, although one primary school in five is offering modern language provision ('*more often than not French*'), the tendency is for languages departments in secondary schools to ignore prior learning and start again. What does this do to pupils' motivation? Has no note been taken of the findings of the Nuffield Primary project of the late 60s and early 70s (Burstall *et al*, 1974)?

Gender difference and motivation?

Another feature of OFSTED reports and other research (see, for example, Barton in Chapter 2) is the worrying discrepancy between boys' and girls' performance in foreign languages. Dobson (1998: 9) points out that 51% of girls and only 35% of boys obtained a higher grade pass (A*–C) in French and that in some schools the difference may be nearly twice as big. Girls predominate in top sets. At A level, boys are heavily outnumbered by girls. This is by no means a reflection of a new trend. Gender and foreign languages has attracted the interest of researchers for some time and in the last 20–30 years in particular (HMI, 1985; Powell, 1979; 1986; Powell and Littlewood, 1983; Powell and Batters, 1986; Clark and Trafford, 1996.) Barton (1997) investigates some of the reasons for boys' inferior performance and these relate to Gardner's **socio-educational model** and Dörnyei's **group-specific motivational components:** their greater propensity to give in to peer pressure; to regard anti-achievement as 'cool'; their unwillingness to suspend belief (especially important in the context of GCSE foreign language learning); their generally inferior listening and reading skills. Barton also helps dispel the myth of languages being perceived as a female subject by boys. Place (1997) and Barton (see Chapter 2) suggest some strategies which may help address the discrepancy in performance between boys and girls, for example:

- emphasis on positive performance rather than negative behaviour;
- attach greater value to speaking;
- overt teaching of organisational skills, 'learning by heart' strategies, revision strategies;
- more emphasis on fact and less on fiction.

What do pupils think?

In the market-driven society in which we live, the perceptions of the consumers (in this case pupils learning foreign languages) are of paramount importance. This is a view supported by Rudduck (1996: 15):

> *If we want to enhance pupils' achievement, why don't we take our agenda for school improvement from their accounts of learning – what helps them to work hard, what switches them off, what kinds of teaching do they value and what kind of support do they need? They are, after all, our expert witnesses.*

Stables and Wikeley (2000) trace a decline in pupils' attitudes to foreign language learning from a high point in the early 1930s when French was regarded as a popular subject. (See Pritchard, 1935. Stables and Stables (1996) identify an upturn in attitudes towards foreign language learning coincidental with increased European integration in 1992 – among first year A level students. If these young people are not positive about their foreign language learning, who will be?) Attitude has an important influence on the nature of an individual's motivation. It reflects the set of values which pupils bring to the foreign language learning experience. These values may be determined by different variables, such as experience of learning the target language, of the target language community, experience of travel, the influence of parents and friends and the attitudes which they demonstrate and articulate. Stables and Wikeley pose the following pertinent question:

> *Given the new emphasis in modern language teaching on communicative competence, on relevance and on role play, and*

> *given the increasing integration of the European Union and the globalisation of the economy, why should the attitudes of English girls and (especially) boys to modern foreign languages seem to be in chronic decline? (op.cit: 29)*

Their research findings lead them to propose the following as possible reasons:

- the perception of the subject importance relates strongly to perceived usefulness for careers (see Marshall Chapter 3);
- modern languages are not seen as enjoyable;
- modern languages are perceived as difficult;
- pedagogical innovations, notably target language teaching and the use of role play, have done nothing to improve pupils' self-images as language learners, and may have done the reverse;
- five years' compulsory learning of one or two languages is too long for pupils without intrinsic or integrative motivation.

So what do pupils tell us about their perceptions of the foreign language learning experience? Research carried out in the 80s and 90s on pupils' response to the foreign language learning experience (see, for example, the work of the Assessment of Performance Unit, DES/DENI/WO, 1985, 86, 87: OXPROD, e.g. Filmer-Sankey, 1983 and 1989; Clark and Trafford, 1996; O'Reilly-Cavani, 1997; Chambers, 1998; Lee *et al,* 1998) reveals considerable congruence in the findings, for example:

- pupils like group- and pair-work and computer-related tasks (although they claim rarely to have this experience in the modern languages classroom);
- they don't like listening activities (which they often perceive as too difficult) or writing (which they often find pointless and boring) or reading aloud;
- they regard the teacher as the greatest influence on their attitude to the classroom experience, be this positive or negative.

The work of Lee *et al,* published in *The Invisible Child* (1998), is particularly interesting because of its focus on those Year 9 pupils who do not stand out in class because of their attainment or behaviour or make particular demands on the teacher's time or attention. They may be categorised as 'average pupils' who simply get on with their work. How often are the motivational implications of their language learning experience missed because of the demands made on teachers by the weaker or the more disruptive or the more able pupils in the class? Refreshingly, 75% of these pupils claim to be as positive about language learning in Year 9 as they were when they started. However, they do have other messages of which note should be taken, if their motivation and probably the motivation of others is to be enhanced:

- the aim of lessons is not always clear; what are they meant to be gaining from them? (See Dobson, 1998 who makes the same observation.) They see value in 'advance organisers', e.g. a guide to the content of the lesson and the related activities written on the board;
- most pupils nominate English as their favourite subject; they enjoy reading, drama, writing stories and poems. So why is this enjoyment not replicated in French, German, Spanish, etc? They are languages just as English is a language. The above activities form part of the French lesson just as they do of the English lesson. Is there not a strong case for increased dialogue, co-operation and collaboration between the English and foreign languages departments?;
- pupils in this sample also claim to enjoy science; they like making things and experimenting. Practical work has a place in the foreign languages classroom. Many of our pupils learn best kinesthetically, yet the tendency is to place most focus on the oral/aural approach (see Marshall, Chapter 3, who reports on the perceived absence of practical work as a reason pupils give for not opting for A level foreign languages);
- pupils claimed to have little idea of their progress or level of attainment (see also Chambers 1999: 147);
- they share OFSTED's perception (see Dobson 1998: 4) of little progress being made from Year 8 onwards; it takes too long to learn a small amount; topics go on for too long;
- they provide little evidence of being equipped to learn (see National Curriculum (DfEE and QCA 1999: 16) on *Developing language-learning skills*). Graddol (1998: 28) stresses the need of the children of the 21st century to be aware of how languages work to enable them to take responsibility for their own learning. Holec provides the principles and practice relating to *Self-directed learning* in the Council of Europe publication: *Strategies in language learning and use*, 1996.

Teachers and motivation

Teachers are up against it. Teachers of modern languages in particular are up against it. They teach a subject seen as irrelevant by many of their pupils. They get little support from a society which traditionally has struggled to see the point of languages although this may be changing: a poll of 1000 people (*Language World Newsletter* December, 1998: 1) revealed that 81% felt that more needed to be done to promote learning of foreign languages; only 14% thought there was no need to learn a foreign language because more and more people speak English. The support they get from Government takes the form of words which are then contradicted by action. (See, for example, on the one hand the promotion of foreign languages in *Towards a national skills agenda* (DfEE, 1999a) and *Labour market and skills trends* (DfEE,1999b), and on the other the implementation of David Blunkett's wish in the revised National Curriculum that more pupils, especially those with a less academic bent and those identified as 'gifted', should be allowed to drop two subjects out of science, modern languages and design and technology. (See also Cassidy, 1999; DfEE 1998b).) They do not often get the support of school management who seem to regard languages as a subject area on the periphery; consider, for example, the place of the second foreign language on most school curricula. (McPake *et al,* 1999: 8, reports that among principal teachers there has been a 37% swing away from support for Languages for All.) How many pupils are given a genuine opportunity to learn two languages beyond Year 9? How often is consideration given to the needs of foreign language teachers and learners by the school timetabler? How often do lessons (often of 70 minutes duration) take place at the end of the day (Chambers, 1992)? How often are foreign languages lessons timetabled to take place in so-called 'temporary classrooms' (situated in the corner of the school playground since 1980)? Teachers want, and are expected, to adopt a multi-media approach. So why are technicians limited to the support of science and technology teachers?

As if all of this were not bad enough, teachers, and teachers of languages in particular, are heavily criticised in the media which seem to have a need to emphasise the negative at every opportunity. Celia Dodd's article in the *Independent* (3 December 1998, *Education* page 8) is one example. It displayed the following headlines:

> *Teacher, I'm bored*
>
> *Why we're so turned off*
>
> *How to make the classroom really dull – Five lessons in tedium*

The following quotations were also highlighted:

> *In a French class, pupils spent an hour and a half going over the present tense with the teacher writing examples on the board and the pupils copying them down.*
>
> *In another French class pupils spent the whole lesson drawing a picture of a table and writing the word 'table' underneath.*

Why do the media feel the need to generalise from a sample of one and to emphasise the negative to the absolute exclusion of any positives?

It is a credit to the teaching profession, and to teachers of foreign languages in particular, that we still have teachers of foreign languages in post. In spite of circumstances militating against them (debt accumulated during undergraduate study; negative media coverage of teaching; the introduction of numeracy, literacy and ICT tests on top of the usual PGCE assessment procedures) graduates still apply for training as teachers of foreign languages, albeit in disturbingly diminishing numbers. O'Reilly-Cavani (1997: 29; see also Chapter 2) accesses the views of teachers who articulate some of the factors above which serve to demotivate them and their pupils and make the following suggestions, *inter alia*:

- teachers should have greater autonomy to teach how and what suits them and their learners best;
- the 'languages for all' policy should be reviewed;
- there is a need for smaller classes;
- the modern languages syllabus and the topics it contains should be reassessed;
- in order to enhance motivation, greater attention should be given to the teaching of culture and grammar.

The National Literacy Strategy (NLS) and its implications for motivation

O'Reilly-Cavani's findings may relate to the Scottish context specifically but may well be generalisable to England. Should this be so, then perhaps mechanisms are already in place to respond to the plea regarding grammar. The National Literacy Strategy has been in place since September 1998 and its influence may feed through in a positive manner to the foreign language learning experience of the pupils. The main strands of the Strategy include:

- a national target that, by 2002, 80% of 11-year olds should reach the standard expected for their age in English (level 4) in the National Curriculum tests for Key Stage 2 (7–11-year olds);
- a *Framework for Teaching* (DfEE, 1998a) which, *inter alia*, sets out termly teaching objectives for the 5–11 range which focus on three broad dimensions of literacy:
  - words level work (phonics, spelling and vocabulary, and also including handwriting);
  - sentence level work (grammar and punctuation);
  - text level work (comprehension and composition).

The implementation of the Strategy has not been trouble free. The educational press (e.g. '*We had another of those horrible Tony Blair English hours*' in *Education Guardian*, 26 January 1999: 4) has been littered with complaints of teachers finding the paperwork unmanageable, of the large amount of extra time it was taking to prepare for the literacy hour, of the weakest pupils struggling to cope and of the strongest being understretched and bored. Such complaints, however, have been counterbalanced by the comments of some parents stressing in response how much their children were enjoying the experience (e.g. '*Don't write off literacy strategy*' in *Education Guardian*, 2 February 1999: 4).

One would normally expect the pay-off for teachers of modern languages, at least on the grammar front, to be positive. It is hoped that we would be in a position to welcome to our classes in Year 7 pupils with the knowledge to distinguish between a verb and a noun. This would be a step forward, in that it would preclude (in theory at least) the investment of time and effort in explaining the meaning of basic grammatical terms which so often contributes to the diminution in motivation and the perception of grammar as something very difficult. This may seem a reasonable expectation but Sue Palmer (1999: 2) urges caution:

> *With the advent of the NLS grammar teaching is back on the agenda. And for primary teachers brought up in an education system in which grammar simply didn't figure, this can be a daunting prospect. Many, unsure of the terminology and of why they are expected to teach it, will do what most of us do when we feel insecure: reach for the worksheets. If this happens, the reintroduction of grammar will be at best a waste of time, at worst counterproductive.*

Grammar aside, there are so many other aspects of the Strategy which complement good practice in Modern Foreign Language teaching and may make a positive contribution to pupils' perceptions of (foreign) language learning and, in turn, their motivation. It can encourage:

- recognition that good oral work plays an important part in the process through which pupils read and compose texts (DfEE, 1998a: 3);
- pupils to orchestrate a full range of reading cues;
- an interest in words and their meanings and a growing vocabulary;
- the ability to plan, draft, revise and edit their own writing;
- development through reading and writing of their powers of imagination, inventiveness and critical awareness (*ibid.*).

None of this is new to the teacher of foreign languages and serves to emphasise the point made earlier, that much is to be gained by dialogue, co-operation and collaboration between the English and Modern Languages departments. (See also Graddol, 1998: 33 and links provided between Modern Languages and English by the revised National Curriculum for each of these subjects.) The Strategy could provide the springboard for this to take place.

The National Literacy Strategy is only one of a number of initiatives which may have a telling influence on the working lives of teachers of languages and the learning experience of their pupils.

The National Grid for Learning (NGFL) and motivation

> *The National Grid for Learning harnesses the power and availability of the Internet to provide a means of connecting and developing the learning society in the information age* (Becta Information Sheet. See www.becta.org.uk/info-sheets/)

Pupils enjoy working with computers (Chambers 1998: 248). They add a motivating dimension to their learning of languages and other subjects. (See Lee *et al*, 1998 where Year 9 pupils articulate the view that working with computers may be enjoyable but not very helpful.) Information technology (IT) gives them some responsibility for their own learning, some autonomy and some opportunity to work at their own pace (Dörnyei's *learner level).* Research findings (e.g. Chambers, op.cit.) also suggest that pupils' experience of IT in foreign languages classes tends to be limited. Why should this be the case? Although access to hardware is improving, this remains a major problem in many Modern Languages departments (Chambers and Higham, 1993. See also Haughton, 2000). In most schools, other subject areas such as business studies, computer studies and mathematics tend to block-book the computer room. The typical modern language department has one or two computers on a trolley which can be used by groups of up to three pupils at a time. This may limit the computer to being used as part of a carousel of activities. Under such conditions it is hardly surprising that teachers do not often feel inclined to make the considerable effort needed to make IT part of the regular foreign language learning/teaching provision.

A common problem is the tendency for teachers to feel they lack the necessary IT competence (Chambers and Higham, 1993). Gunn (1998: 8), for example, stated that '*teachers lacked the training and support to be fully effective in the use of IT*'. A certain degree of confidence in one's own ability and familiarity with the hard- and software are necessary before basing a lesson for up to 30 pupils on an IT package or an Internet search.

The NGFL can do little about the problem of access to hardware; nor is it its role to provide teachers with competence and confidence-enhancing training. (The latter is the responsibility of the Government's New Opportunity Fund (NOF) and the Teacher Training Agency (TTA) who are supervising the £230 million training scheme to help Britain's 400,000 teachers become proficient in ICT by 2002. CILT is the only provider approved to run courses specifically and uniquely for modern languages teachers. (For further information contact CILT.) The NGFL includes the aim, however, to provide personal e-mail addresses for half the nation's pupils by 2002. This opens up all sorts of opportunities on the foreign language learning front. All those references in the National Curriculum (e.g. DfEE and QCA 1999: 17, 30, 34) to use e-mail may become a real possibility as opposed to an ideal, achievable only in the best resourced schools. For years we have been promoting the motivational importance of learners writing for a real readership, of reading, listening and speaking for a real reason. The Internet provides an accessible opportunity for this. (See Lamb and Fisher, 1999 on the use of internet-based activities on the World Cup.) The NGFL will provide:

> *... a network of inter-connected web sites and education services based on the Internet which will provide content to support teaching, learning, training and administration in schools, colleges, universities, libraries, the workplace and the home; a resource for everyone enhancing educational standards, literacy, numeracy and subject knowledge; a way of finding and using on-line learning and teaching materials (op.cit.)*

The Nuffield Languages Inquiry (NLI) and its implications for motivation

> *... in a century which has been characterised by explosive growth in the technology of travel and communication, we have had to wait until the last moments before the new millennium to take an overall strategic look at our power as a nation to communicate adequately with speakers of other languages. (Moys, 1998: 4)*

The NLI offered the opportunity to review where we stood with regard to Modern Foreign Languages in this country. It posed the following questions:

1. *What capability in languages will this country need in the next 20 years if it is to fulfil its economic, strategic, social and cultural aims and responsibilities, and the aspirations of its citizens?*
2. *To what extent do present policies and arrangements meet these needs?*
3. *What strategic planning and initiatives will be required in the light of the present position? (ibid.)*

As Moys suggested above, it was high time that these important questions were tackled seriously and meaningfully.

Among the Inquiry's main findings were these:

- *people are looking for leadership to improve the nation's capability in languages;*
- *young people from the UK are at a disadvantage in the recruitment market;*
- *the UK needs competence in many languages – not just French – but the education system is not geared up to achieve this;*
- *the government has no coherent approach to languages;*
- *in spite of parental demand, there is still no UK-wide agenda for children to start languages early;*

- *secondary school pupils lack motivation or direction;*
- *nine out of ten children stop learning languages at 16;*
- *university language departments are closing, leaving the sector in deep crisis;*
- *the UK desperately needs more language teachers.*

(*Nuffield Languages Inquiry*, 2000a: 4–5)

Many of these findings came as no surprise. 'What can be done to address the issues?' was the question which it was hoped the report would address. These were some of its proposals:

- languages should be designated a key skill with the same status as literacy, numeracy and ICT;
- a languages supremo should be appointed, attached to the Cabinet Office and with direct access to the Prime Minister;
- languages should be given an enhanced profile;
- children should learn languages from age seven;
- the status of languages in schools should be enhanced; the range of languages on offer should be increased; more flexible approaches to teaching should be adopted, including wider use of ICT;
- *a language should be a requirement for university entry and for designated vocational qualifications;*
- the organisation and funding of languages in higher education should be reformed;
- radical short-term measures should be implemented to help teacher recruitment.

(*op.cit.*: 6–7)

The publication of the report was accompanied by the fanfare it deserved. It was given a position of prominence by all areas of the media. Time only will tell whether its proposals will be taken seriously. We who have a love for languages and who recognise their importance must do what we can to ensure that the report retains a place in the public consciousness and is not allowed to gather dust on the shelf.

So what can we do about motivation?

The following chapters attempt to offer some ideas on how to answer the above question. The authors provide concrete examples and their rationale. You may not be able to drop the examples provided straight into tomorrow's Year 9 lesson, but the thinking behind the examples may well provide you with stimuli to adapt your approach to meet the specific needs of your classes.

The book is divided into two parts:

1. chapters focusing on Dörnyei's **Learning situation level**
2. chapters focusing on Dörnyei's **Learner level**

This does not mean that Dörnyei's **Language level** is ignored or irrelevant. On the contrary, it permeates both sections. It must also be acknowledged that no clearcut distinction exists between the two sections of the book. While a given chapter may, on balance, give more attention to one of the two named levels, issues relating to the other levels and indeed to Gardner's *socio-educational model* may also be included.

Dörnyei's Learning situation level

Chapter 1: What can be learned from a survey conducted in Glasgow? Jane O'Reilly-Cavani summarises the views of pupils on their attitudes to foreign language learning, their likes and dislikes.

Chapter 2: The gender debate. Amanda Barton looks at the difference in boys' and girls' perceptions of foreign languages and the learning experience.

Chapter 3: Where have all the sixth form foreign language learners gone? Why are they not opting for A level? Keith Marshall comes up with some answers and some suggestions on what can be done about the problem.

Chapter 4: What if a project was carried out which focused on the teaching and learning of more able pupils? Would this have a beneficial effect on the other pupils too? David Stork tests the hypothesis in the East Riding of Yorkshire.

Chapter 5: A success story. The phoenix rises from the ashes. An interview with Susan Chamberlain who adopted a languages department in the doldrums. She describes how she and her colleagues turned things around. This is followed by an interview with Steven Fawkes who had a significant influence on Susan. What can we learn from him about his approach and the thinking that underpins it? What are the resources that do the trick?

Chapter 6: Jim McElwee does not make us salivate at the idea of the latest hard- and software, which we are unlikely to have in the forseeable future, but rather looks at the basics. He moves the pupils on from 'mindless clicking' to meaningful learning.

Dörnyei's Learner level

Chapter 7: Terry Lamb describes how the foreign language learning ball can and must be put into the pupil's court. He draws on his own experience of working with disaffected pupils.

Chapter 8: Kim Brown adopts a strategy with a practical dimension which promotes an autonomous approach to foreign language learning with a Year 8 and a Year 10 class. Have you ever tried a sunflower project to facilitate pupils' learning?

Chapter 9: Jenifer Alison shows how she provides her pupils with a reason to learn a foreign language by providing a vocational framework. An insight into how learning French can be made relevant to pupils who traditionally struggle to see the point of it all.

Chapter 10: Primary Foreign Languages – have we moved on since Nuffield? Have things changed around the Key Stage 2–3 transfer point? Ann Gregory provides some answers based on her experience in North Yorkshire.

Chapter 11: This concluding chapter is Janus-like in looking backward and forward. What have we learned? Where do we go from here? What should the future hold?

By the end of the book, we may find ourselves in a position to change things for the better. A review of approaches to foreign language teaching throughout the centuries provides an image of a pendulum swinging back and forth, of wheels being reinvented, of babies being thrown out with the bathwater. The contributors to this book focus on pupil-motivation to show a way to break the mould.

Bibliography

Asher C, 'Patterns and trends in vacancies for basic scale Modern Foreign Language teaching posts, 1983–1998' in *Language Learning Journal*, 20: 66–73 (1999)

Barton A, Boys' under-achievement in GCSE modern languages: reviewing the reasons' in *Language Learning Journal*, 16: 11–16 (1997)

Bialystok E, 'A theoretical model of second language learning' in *Language learning*, 28: 69–83 (1978)

Boaks P, 'Languages in schools' in Nuffield Languages Inquiry *Where are we going with languages?*, pp34–43 (Nuffield Foundation, 1998)

Burstall C, S Cohen, M Hargreaves and M Jamieson, Primary *French in the Balance*, (NFER 1974)

Cannon W, *The Wisdom of the Body*, (New York: Norton, 1932)

Carroll J, 'Conscious and automatic processes in language learning' in *Canadian Modern Language Review*, 37: 462–74 (1981)

Cassidy S, 'Talented pupils can opt out of GCSEs' in *Times Educational Supplement*, 23 July, p.2 (1999)

Chambers G, 'Modern languages and the timetable' in *Language Learning Journal*, 5: 55–59 (1992)

Chambers G, 'Pupils' perceptions of the foreign language learning experience' in *Language Teaching Research*, Vol.2, 3: 231–259 (1998)

Chambers G, *Motivating language learners* (Multilingual Matters, 1999)

Chambers G and J Higham, 'Information technology: the school dimension' in *Information Technology in Initial Teacher Education: the modern languages perspective*, (National Council for Educational Technology, 1993)

Clark A and J Trafford, 'Return to gender: boys' and girls' attitudes and achievements' in *Language Learning Journal*, 14: 40–49 (1996)

Clément R, 'Ethnicity, contact and communicative competence in a second language' in Giles H, W Robinson and P Smith (eds), *Language: social psychological perspectives*, (Pergamon, 1980)

DES/DENI/WO, *Foreign Language Performance in Schools: a report on the 1983 survey of French*, (HMSO, APU, 1985)

DES/DENI/WO, *Foreign Language Performance in Schools: a report on the 1984 survey of French, German and Spanish*, (HMSO, APU, 1986)

DES/DENI/WO, *Foreign Language Performance in Schools: a report on the 1985 survey of French, German and Spanish*, (HMSO, APU, 1987)

DfE/WO, *Modern Foreign Languages in the National Curriculum*, (HMSO, 1995)

DfEE, *The National Literacy Strategy: Framework for Teaching*, (DfEE, 1998a)

DfEE, *The Education (National Curriculum) (Exceptions at Key Stage 4) Regulations 1998 (Statutory Instruments 1998 No 2021)* (DfEE, 1998b)

DfEE, *Towards a national skills agenda*, (DfEE, 1999a)

DfEE, *Labour market and skills trends*, (DfEE, 1999b)

DfEE and QCA, *Modern foreign languages: The National Curriculum for England* (DfEE and QCA, 1999)

Dobson A, *Modern Foreign Languages Inspected*, (CILT, 1998)

Dörnyei Z, 'Motivation and Motivating in the Foreign Language Classroom' *in The Modern Language Journal*,78, iii: 273–284 (1994)

Dörnyei Z, 'Motivation in second and foreign language learning' in *Language Teaching*, 31: 117–135 (1998)

Dörnyei Z and I Ottó, 'Motivation in action: A process model of L2 motivation' in *Working Papers in Applied Linguistics*, 4: 43–69 (Thames Valley University, 1998)

Downes P, '¿Qué?' in *Times Educational Supplement*, 5 March, pp18–19 (1999)

Filmer-Sankey C, *A Study of First-Year Pupils' Attitudes towards French, German and Spanish*, (OXPROD, 1989)

Filmer-Sankey C, *A Study of Second-Year Pupils' Attitudes towards French, German and Spanish*, (OXPROD, 1991)

Gardner R, *Social Psychology and Second Language Learning*, (Arnold, 1985)

Giles H and J Byrne, 'An intergroup approach to second language acquisition' in *Journal of Multilingual and Multicultural Development*, 1: 17–40 (1982)

Gill C, 'One will not add up in a world market' in *Times Educational Supplement*, 5 March, p19 (1999)

Graddol D, 'Will English be enough?' in *Where are we going with languages?*, pp24–33 (Nuffield Foundation, 1998)

Gunn O, 'Excellence for all children. Meeting Special Educational Needs' in *Teaching Today*, 19: 8–9 (1998)

Hagen S, 'What does global trade mean for UK languages?' in in *Where are we going with languages?*, pp14–23 (Nuffield Foundation, 1998)

Haughton E, 'Hurdles for screen stars' in *Guardian Education*, 15.2., p.5 (2000)

HMI, Boys and modern languages, (HMSO, 1985)

Holec H, D Little and R Richterich, *Strategies in language learning and use*, (Strasbourg: Council of Europe, 1996)

Hull C, *A behaviour system and principles of behaviour* (New York: Yale University Press, 1943)

Jones S, 'How does Europe promote languages?' in *Where are we going with languages?*, pp6–13 (Nuffield Foundation, 1998)

Jung J, *Understanding Human Motivation*, (Macmillan, 1978)

Krashen S, 'The monitor model for second language acquisition' in Gingras R, (ed) *Second-language acquisition and foreign language teaching* (Arlington, Virginia: Center for Applied Linguistics 1978)

Krashen S, *Second language acquisition and second language learning*, (Pergamon 1981)

Krashen S, *Principles and Practice in Second Language Acquisition* (Pergamon 1982)

Lamb T and J Fisher, 'Making connections: football, the internet and reluctant language learners' in *Language Learning Journal*, in press (2000)

Lambert W, 'Psychological approaches to the study of language Part I: On learning, thinking and human abilities' in *Modern Language Journal*, 14: 51–62 (1963a)

Lambert W, 'Psychological approaches to the study of language Part II: On second language learning and bilingualism' in *Modern Language Journal*,14: 114-121 (1963b)

Lambert W, 'A social psychology of bilingualism' in *Journal of Social Issues*, 23: 91-109 (1967)

Lambert W, 'Culture and language as factors in learning and education' in Aboud F and R Meade (eds), *Cultural factors in learning and education*, (Bellingham, Washington: Fifth Western Washington Symposium on Learning, 1974)

Lee, J, Buckland, D and G Shaw *The Invisible Child* (CILT, 1998)

McPake J, R Johnstone, L Low and L Lyall, *Interchange 59: Foreign Languages in the Upper Secondary School: A Study of the Causes of Decline*, (Scottish Office Education and Industry Department, 1999)

Moys A, 'Where are we going with languages?' in *Where are we going with languages?*, pp4–5 (Nuffield Foundation, 1998)

NCC, *Modern Foreign Languages Non-Statutory Guidance*, (NCC, 1992)

Nuffield Languages Inquiry, *Languages: the next generation; a summary of the final report of the Nuffield Languages Inquiry*, (Nuffield Languages Foundation, 2000a)

Nuffield Languages Inquiry, *Languages: the next generation; the final report and recommendations of the Nuffield Languages Inquiry*, (Nuffield Languages Foundation, 2000b)

O'Reilly-Cavani J, *Glasgow Schools' Language Learning and Teaching Project*, (City of Glasgow and University of Glasgow, 1997)

Palmer S, 'Find your feet in the grammar minefield' in *Times Educational Supplement*, 22 January, p.20 (1999)

Place D, 1997 'Boys will be boys – boys and under-achievement in MFL' in *Language Learning Journal*, 16: 3–10 (1997)

Powell R, 'Sex differences and language learning: a review of the evidence' in *Audio-Visual Language Journal*, 17 (1): 19–24 (1979)

Powell R and J Batters, 'Sex of Teacher and the Image of Foreign Languages in Schools' in *Educational Studies*,12 (3): 245–254 (1986)

Powell R and P Littlewood, 'Why choose French? Boys' and Girls' attitudes at the Option Stage' in *British Journal of Language Teaching*, 21 (1): 36–39,44 (1983)

Pritchard R, 'The relative popularity of secondary school subjects at various ages' in *British Journal of Educational Psychology*, 5: 157–179 (1935)

QCA/DfEE, *The review of the national curriculum in England. The consultation materials*, (QCA, 1999)

QCA/DfEE, *The review of the national curriculum in England. The Secretary of State's proposals*, (QCA, 1999)

Rudduck J, 'Testimony of the expert witnesses' in *Times Educational Supplement*, 28 June, p.15 (1996)

Skinner B, *Verbal Behaviour* (New York: Appleton-Century-Croft, 1957)

Schumann J, 'The acculturation model for second language acquisition' in Gingras R, *Second language acquisition and foreign language teaching* (Arlington V.A.: Center for Applied Linguistics, 1978a)

Schumann J, 'Social and psychological factors in second language acquisition' in Richards J, (ed) *Understanding second and foreign language learning* (Rowley, Mass.: Newbury House, 1978b)

Stables A and S Stables, 'Modern languages at A level: the danger of curricular discontinuity' in *Language Learning Journal*, 14: 50–52 (1996)

Stables A and F Wikeley, 'From bad to worse? Pupils' attitudes to modern foreign languages at ages 14 and 15' in *Language Learning Journal*, No.20, in press (2000)

Towell R, 'Languages in Higher Education' in *Where are we going with languages?*, pp44–53 (Nuffield Foundation, 1998)

Weiner B, *Theories of Motivation*, (Chicago: Rand McNally College Publishing Company, 1972)

Weiner B, *Human Motivation* (New York: Holt, Rinehart and Winston, 1980)

PART ONE

Dörnyei's Learning Situation Level

Course-specific motivational components – this relates to the motivational influence of the syllabus, teaching materials, teaching methods, learning activities.

Teacher-specific motivational components – this relates to the teacher-pupil relationship, the teacher's approach to behaviour management, the promotion of 'sharing' of ideas and views between pupils as well as teacher and pupils, the provision of motivating feedback.

Group-specific motivational components – the promotion of collaboration; shared goals; shared norms of behaviour.

Chapter 1

Motivation in language learning: a Glasgow snapshot

Jane O'Reilly Cavani

Jane O'Reilly Cavani looks at motivation from the pupils' perspective. Within a teaching context which displays many of the worrying characteristics to which most of us can relate, the pupils help her to identify a number of positive features and some negative, covering many aspects of Dörnyei's framework. How can the positives be built upon and the challenge of tackling the negatives be taken up?

Background

Poor Standard Grade results in the one compulsory MFL studied, little or no uptake for a second MFL and low uptake for the Higher in a MFL. This situation clearly represented a problem for all levels of the Scottish education system, as well as for pupils and employers via the potential restriction of career opportunities.

The present study constitutes an account of the research conducted by the University of Glasgow French Department, focusing in particular on S1 to S6[1] Glasgow City pupils' attitudes and levels of motivation with regard to this MFL teaching and learning situation.

Research design

Data collected concentrated on the following areas:

- a survey of all Glasgow City Modern Languages Departments to facilitate the selection of four sample schools by the Languages Adviser of Glasgow City Council;[2]

- interviews with sample school principal teachers of modern languages in order to compile school profiles and gather teacher views;
- observation of S1 and S2 French classes in Terms 1 and 3 – shadowing and audio-recording one S1 and one S2 French class in each school for four periods over a two-week time span, concentrating on a number of areas relating to the curriculum, resources and teaching and learning;
- pupil survey in Term 2 aiming to access pupil attitudes and levels of motivation.

The last aspect represented the central phase in the active collection of primary data from the classroom. It involved pupils of both genders from each year group S1 to S6 in order to gauge attitudinal changes and gender differences towards French as pupils progressed through secondary education. There were two strands:

Quantitative

A questionnaire was distributed to one French class from each year group S1 to S4 and to all S5/S6 French pupils in each sample school. A total of 294 pupils participated in the survey. To ensure standardisation of implementation, the filling in of the questionnaires was administered by the project research assistant. The questionnaire comprised primarily quantifiable, dichotomous and multiple-choice questions, with a small number of open questions providing a certain amount of qualitative data. It was also slightly adapted to suit the different learning circumstances of pupils in the lower secondary, pupils preparing for Standard Grade and pupils preparing for Higher Grade or National Certificate modules.

Qualitative

Audio-recorded, semi-structured interviews were carried out in each of the sample schools with a group of six pupils from each year group S1 to S4 and six pupils from S5/S6. A quota sampling technique was used, whereby the individuals to be interviewed were selected on the basis of strict criteria – in this case gender and ability, the latter as determined by the class teacher on the basis of classroom performance and assessments.[3] In addition, other factors were taken into consideration: the S3 and S4 groups contained at least one pupil studying a second MFL, and the S5/S6 groups comprised both French continuers (at both Higher and National Certificate Module level where possible) and non-continuers. This selection process helped to ensure that the final sample of pupils was as representative as possible despite the small number of sample schools being visited. The method implemented (see Kent, 1996 for a similar approach) was designed to elicit spontaneous written responses from the pupils, followed by a conversation covering ground relating to those anonymous comments.[4] The data collected were transcribed and analysed in detail from a qualitative perspective.

Pupil motivation: findings from the survey

Dörnyei's (1994) three levels were exploited as a framework for analysing and reporting some of the findings of the survey conducted in the three Glasgow sample schools:

- the language level
- the learner level
- the learning situation level

These levels are further defined as follows:

> *The three levels coincide with the three basic constituents of the L2 learning process (the L2, the L2 learner, and the L2 learning environment) and also reflect the three different aspects of language mentioned earlier (the social dimension, the personal dimension, and the educational subject matter dimension).* (Dörnyei, 1994: 279)

Language level

It was possible to analyse the responses of the Glasgow pupils in both the questionnaire and the semi-structured discussion group from the point of view of the two components of language level motivation as defined by Dörnyei: integrativeness and instrumentality.[5]

- Integrativeness

  Many Glasgow pupils did express a wish to draw closer to the French community and its culture. While on average[6] only a third of pupils had visited France before (with a high proportion of them only passing through), an average of 68% expressed a positive attitude towards finding out about France. Indeed, in the course of the discussion groups it emerged that pupils tended to have a positive, if somewhat stereotypical and relatively uninformed, attitude towards France. Thus it would appear that the inclusion of cultural elements in coursework may be a motivating factor.

- Instrumentality

  Glasgow pupils also appeared to appreciate the overall usefulness of learning French. On average 89% of pupils surveyed felt that learning French or any foreign language was generally useful. However, if we dissect this general view, we find that there was a variety of future goals, each generating a range of different attitudes.

  In the short-term, an examination pass was a major goal, but only up to a certain level:

I'd like to have it as a qualification if I went for a job. (S2 Girl)

Just to get a Standard Grade. (S5 Girl)

However, French was viewed as being a difficult subject, particularly in S4 and S5/S6, with very few pupils wishing or opting to continue post-Standard Grade: on average only 4% of pupils in the three sample schools who could have studied French in S5/S6 had actually opted to do so. Comments were made on the level of difficulty and the amount of work required:

You need to work harder at it. (S4 Girl)

It's probably the hardest subject I'm doing just now. (S4 Boy)

I don't really think I could have coped with doing the French stuff and my other Highers as well. (S5 Girl)

In the short to long-term, holidays represented a possible motivating factor, although there were comments about not wishing to study the language in too much depth:

I'd like to learn just a wee bit, just some of the stuff I'd need, not the stuff I wouldn't. (S1 Boy)

This may represent yet another reason for not continuing post-Standard Grade. Many pupils also felt that France was not a likely holiday destination for them and that other languages would be more useful:

I wouldn't really go to France as much as I would go to Spain. (S1 Girl)

[French] doesn't interest a lot of people you know. Some people think 'I'll never be going to France, I won't need it.' (S5 Boy)

Indeed, approximately one third of questionnaire respondents expressed an interest in studying either Italian or Spanish instead of French. It is therefore clear that diversified language provision was viewed positively by many pupils.

In the longer-term, future career was identified as a potential motivating factor, but again only to a limited extent. Questionnaire returns revealed that, on average, almost three quarters of pupils felt that studying a foreign language would help them get a job, while a similar proportion expected to use a foreign language in a job at some point. However, almost three quarters of pupils thought that most businesses in Europe use English as their main language, with only just over half of pupils believing that businesses actively recruit people who study a foreign language.

Learner level

Dörnyei (1994) highlights two main components in relation to the learner, both of which can be illustrated using findings from the Glasgow survey:

- Need for achievement

  In order to feel motivated to learn a MFL, pupils must have a set of goals in sight and feel that they are making progress towards achieving those goals. Comments made by Glasgow pupils in the discussion groups revealed that many of them were unaware of any programme of work to be followed, beyond working through the coursebook, and consequently felt lost:

  > *We just work through all the chapters in the book.* (S1 Girl)
  >
  > *It seems as if we just come in and it's like, 'We'll just do this today'* . (S5 Girl)

  It is important to stress that goals should be carefully negotiated: challenging but achievable.

  An average of 20% of those who completed the questionnaire (as well as one third of those interviewed) described French as boring, with the level of negativity gradually increasing from year group to year group to reach a peak in S4 of over 50% of the male respondents. '*Boring*' was defined by the sample pupils in different ways: for some pupils it meant that the goals set were not challenging enough and the methods used to achieve them too repetitive, such as the rote-learning of vocabulary and grammar: '*It was the same all the time, every period*' (S5 Boy), while for others it meant too difficult, with the imagined ultimate goal of native speaker fluency appearing totally out of reach.

- Self-confidence

  Clearly self-confidence also has a major role to play in encouraging any pupil to stay on the path leading towards their ultimate goal. In the Glasgow project the majority of questionnaire respondents expressed a dislike for any activity involving individual performance, such as reading aloud to the class or acting out a conversation, thus demonstrating their anxiety about language use.

Learning situation level

Here Dörnyei highlights three main components in relation to the learning situation, each of which can again be illustrated using findings from the Glasgow survey:

- Course-specific

Clearly courses should be of interest and relevance to pupils. This, however, is one area where pupils expressed certain reservations. In both the questionnaire returns and the discussion groups, the most frequently criticised aspects of learning French included dated material, irrelevant content (particularly when focused on self) and non-stimulating or anxiety-inducing methods, such as rote-learning or individual performance. Pupils did, on the other hand, praise directly relevant and challenging content (learning about France for example), stimulating materials based on new technologies (computers, videos) and confidence-boosting methods.

- Teacher-specific

The importance of the teacher as a motivating force became very apparent in the Glasgow pupils' questionnaire returns. When asked to give their favourite school subject and a reason for liking it, the entire range of subjects was mentioned with the influence of the teacher most often cited as the major influential factor. Teachers who led the class supportively, presented tasks clearly and enthusiastically and gave feedback constructively, inspired the greatest level of participation among pupils: '*The teacher doesn't shout at you if you get an answer wrong. The class is relaxed but gets work done*' (S3 Girl). These views were reiterated in the discussion groups:

> *Be a friendly teacher, one you're not scared to ask for help or put your hand up if you don't understand. (S3 Boy)*

> *The teacher who makes it interesting is a good teacher. (S5 Boy)*

- Group-specific

The potential negative influence of group composition and peer pressure became evident in pupils' comments. For many, liking a *difficult* subject such as French was *square*, and it was therefore not to be chosen post-Standard Grade: '*People were just going with the flow. Cos other people didn't like it, they didn't like it.*' (S5 Boy)

Group influence could also be positive: pupils cited drama as a favourite subject because the anxiety-inducing, performance-based aspect was offset by a motivating dimension based on group goals and group cohesion: '*You do it all in a group. It's not like you're in front of everybody. It's a few of you working together.*' (S1 Boy)

The next step: improving motivation

Research aimed at addressing a given problem should ideally lead to innovation aimed at providing a solution. Sally Brown gives an excellent description of what such innovation ought to be in a classroom context, stressing that top-down decisions without consultation are to be avoided if effective change is to take place:

> *As educators we must always be thinking about improvements, and [...] if change is to occur it has to be introduced at the front-line where teacher and learner meet. Sophisticated efforts at innovation in the great halls of power and policy are a waste of time unless they can be sold to those with the responsibility for implementing the changes. That means that the language of innovation has to interlock with the ways in which teachers make sense of their classroom world, just as the language teachers use in the classroom has to engage with the ways in which pupils make sense of their worlds.* (Brown 1996: 80)

It was felt, therefore, that if there was to be any hope of reversing the continuing disaffection with modern languages among Scottish pupils, then all teachers, as well as pupils, had to feel involved in the search for possible solutions. A number of Glasgow initiatives have attempted to do just that:

Glasgow teachers' consultation forum

Following the Glasgow Project, the University of Glasgow offered to provide a forum to enable modern languages teachers both to share their perceptions of current problems and to present materials or give an account of practices which they felt had worked effectively. Regular meetings have been taking place since autumn 1997, and have addressed a wide range of issues:

- primary-secondary liaison;
- grammar teaching;
- the introduction of the new post-16 examination system in Scotland (Higher Still);
- the use of Information and Communication Technology (ICT) in the MFL classroom.

ICT projects

The Glasgow Project found that there was undoubtedly room for improvement in the area of resources in all of the participating schools. In particular it was felt that easier access to computers and video facilities would permit the introduction of new teaching approaches, which may in turn increase pupil motivation, particularly given that this was an area highlighted by pupils themselves: *kind of exciting*, *more fun*, and *a pure laugh* were just a few of the comments made about computer-assisted language learning in the course of the discussion groups.

Thus a follow-on pilot project was launched in Glasgow City in early 1998 '*to explore the use of ICT, and in particular Internet-based resources, for the teaching of French in Glasgow schools*'. This project has revealed that further staff training and on-going support are essential. It is, nevertheless, hoped that it will be possible to identify resources to be used by teachers and pupils, and to pilot their integration within courses with a view to developing and demonstrating effective use.

Individual teachers in individual schools have also made an effort to improve motivation via the use of ICT resources. In 1999, for example, a teacher in East Renfrewshire, a local authority area adjacent to Glasgow City, launched a MFL web-site, the main aim of which is to provide a forum where learners and educators alike can access resources for learning and teaching in several languages and at several levels (Pentleton, 1999).

Conclusion

The small-scale Glasgow research project succeeded in revealing certain aspects of pupil motivation at the local level, and resulted in a series of initiatives aimed at improving this important element of MFL learning and teaching, again at the local level.

However, local initiatives alone are not a panacea. The importance of the recommendations produced by the Foreign Languages in the Upper Secondary School research into the decline in uptake (see McPake *et al*, 1999: 73–81) cannot be overstated. This research identified the following as possible explanations for numbers opting for modern languages at Higher level:

- *critical views on teaching and learning methods used in schools, particularly in S3 and S4;*
- *restrictions on uptake of modern languages at S2 and S4 resulting from school options and choices systems, and also from restrictions commonly operated by modern languages departments themselves, to ensure that only able students continue modern language study to Higher level;*
- *lack of promotion of modern languages by modern languages departments, by guidance staff or, more generally, by the school 'ethos'.*

The research also explored the following explanations for pupils' poor motivation:

- *students' experiences of language learning are not intrinsically rewarding;*
- *students are not interested in other languages and cultures;*
- *students see no material gain for themselves in learning another language;*
- *the expectations students have of themselves as language learners are not met and their confidence in their linguistic ability is not high.*

The recommendations to tackle the above issues include the following:

- *consideration should be given to enhancing work-related elements within the S3 and S4 courses;*
- *modern languages departments should become more actively involved in the promotion of their own subject, focusing on the potential of languages to support and enhance study in a variety of areas in Higher Education, or in career development;*
- *guidance teachers' attention should be drawn to changing patterns of modern language teaching in higher education, where languages are increasingly linked to 'professional' subjects such as business studies, accountancy, law etc, and where extensive opportunities for study and work experience in Europe are now available;*
- *guidance teachers should be encouraged to see the world of work within Europe rather than just within Scotland as their remit;*
- *modern languages teachers and guidance staff should ensure that they are well informed of the opportunities for using languages for study and work experience abroad, and that they pass this information on to students;*
- *'role models' should be sought at local and national level to encourage students to become aware of the long-term value of achieving and maintaining competence in a foreign language;*
- *bodies with an interest in promoting labour mobility within Europe should encourage higher education institutions and employers' organisations to publicise opportunities for study and work abroad in their recruitment literature, pointing out the value of competence in a foreign language.*

Something must be done to disperse the *climate of negativity* now so prevalent among pupils, teachers and the wider society, and initiate the all-important process of '*fostering students' positive attitudes towards their second language learning situation at the earliest possible time*' (Naiman *et al*, 1996: 147).

We must do our best to promote the positive feelings that MFL learning can and does engender in pupils at all levels, so that more would echo the words of one Glasgow S1 girl: '*[French] is useful if you go abroad. It is really fun. The teacher is cool*'.

Cavani exploits Dörnyei's framework to reflect how pupils provide a mixed message on their French learning experience. On the positive side:

- they have a relatively positive attitude to French;
- they appreciate the usefulness of learning French;
- they enjoy the variety of media (videos; ICT).

On the less positive side:

- they find the learning of French boring and routine;
- they find it anxiety inducing – i.e. because of reading aloud and acting out dialogues;
- they find French more difficult than other subjects;
- they find materials out of date and irrelevant.

The problems cannot be tackled by individual schools or individual LEAs. Collaboration is the key. Motivation can be enhanced by working together in the development and sharing of materials on Dörnyei's three levels:

- the learning situation level – to produce appropriate attractive teaching materials, involving a variety of media; to help teachers develop strategies for providing positive feedback and bolstering self-esteem and promote a positive learning environment;
- the language level – to promote the relevance and usefulness of foreign languages;
- the learner level – to enhance the perception of the language learning experience.

Bibliography

Brown S, 'Teaching, learning and the learning environment' in *Language Learning Journal*, 14: 80–84 (1996)

Dörnyei Z, 'Motivation and Motivating in the Foreign Language Classroom' in *The Modern Language Journal*, 78: 273–84 (1994)

Gardner R and W Lambert, *Attitudes and Motivation in Second Language Learning* (Newbury House, 1972)

Kent D, *An investigation into the factors influencing the learning of foreign languages in S5 and S6 in Scottish school* (Department of Education, University of Stirling, 1996)

McPake J, R Johnstone, L Low and L Lyall, *Foreign Languages in the Upper Secondary School: A Study of the Causes of Decline* (SCRE, 1999)

Naiman N, M Fröhlich, H Stern and A Todesco, *The Good Language Learner* (Multilingual Matters, 1996)

O'Reilly-Cavani J and R Birks, *Glasgow Schools Language Learning and Teaching Project: Final Report* (University of Glasgow, 1997)

Pentleton M, www.linguaweb@ndirect.co.uk (1999)

SOED – Scottish Office Education Department, *Curriculum and Assessment in Scotland, National Guidelines: Modern European Languages 5–14* (SOED, 1993)

Notes

1 All six years of Scottish secondary education (Years 8 to 13).

2 Unfortunately problems encountered at the survey stage of the research led to the withdrawal of one of the schools from the project at the start of the second term. It should be stressed, therefore, that the small number of schools involved in the University of Glasgow research (only 3 schools out of 39) necessarily limits the statistical significance of the findings. In many respects the research carried out in the sample schools may be better described as a series of case studies rather than as a true quantitative and qualitative survey.

3 Three boys and three girls were included in each discussion group (apart from S5/S6 where this was not always possible): a boy and a girl of higher ability, a boy and a girl of middle ability and a boy and a girl of lower ability.

4 The University of Glasgow procedure, while similar, since pupils' spontaneous reactions were written down, read aloud and discussed in turn, differed slightly in that the interview was not unstructured, but semi-structured: pupils responded not to a verbal comment, but to simple visual stimuli (flashcards bearing first the word *France*, and later the words *French classes*) while at the same time being guided through a number of topics previously defined by the research team.

5 Dörnyei thus reiterates Oxford and Shearin's desire *to maintain the best of the existing L2 learning motivation theory and push its parameters outwards*. Hence his retention of these two fundamental components of Gardner and Lambert's theory: integrativeness defined as *a positive disposition towards the L2 group*, and instrumentality as *the potential pragmatic gains of L2 proficiency* (Dörnyei, 1994: 274).

6 It should be noted that any questionnaire return statistics qualified as *average* refer to the proportion or percentage of all 294 questionnaire respondents drawn from across all year groups. This was felt to be appropriate given the absence of any huge discrepancy between year groups.

Chapter 2

Gender differences in pupils' perceptions of modern foreign languages

Amanda Barton

How big a motivational issue is gender in modern languages teaching and learning? What can we do about it? In answering these questions Amanda Barton examines some of the areas also seen as important by Dörnyei:

- pupils' perception of the relevance of modern languages (Learning Situation Level – course specific motivational components)
- pupils' perception of modern languages as a subject for girls (group-specific components)

and in addition

- contact with native speakers (Language Level)
- pupils' estimation of their own ability (Learner Level)

Introduction

This chapter describes the findings of doctoral research which set out to explore the reasons why so many boys fail to achieve their full potential in modern foreign languages. The research involved working with five UK secondary schools which were endeavouring to raise pupils' achievement in the subject through piloting single-sex initiatives:

- two inner-city mixed comprehensive schools;
- one school located in a large town which had two single-sex grammar schools;
- a grant-maintained school within the commuter belt of a large city;
- one school located in a semi-rural area and served a large catchment area which included a university.

A case study approach was adopted to take account of the diverse features that characterised each individual school and group. The data was collected over a two-year period, from 1996–98, by means of interviews and informal discussion with pupils and staff, a range of questionnaires and classroom observation.

Although the research set out to analyse how single-sex grouping might influence pupils' learning of modern foreign languages, it soon became clear that the pupils' perspectives were moulded by a complex myriad of variables, rather than merely by the grouping. The findings described here are derived principally from interviews and from a questionnaire which was administered in 1997 to 799 pupils in both mixed and single-sex groups. This questionnaire sought to examine variables such as:

- pupils' genderised perceptions of the subject;
- their social and cultural background;
- their views on the importance and relevance of language learning.

Those variables which emerged as most significant are analysed here in relation to differences between boys' and girls' perceptions. Such differences might help to explain why the gender disparity in performance continues to characterise foreign language learning to an alarming degree.

Pupils' enjoyment of modern foreign languages

The disparity between boys' and girls' attitudes to modern foreign languages has frequently been described in research literature (Burstall, 1974; Batters, 1988; Powell, 1986; Loulidi, 1990; Aplin, 1991) and is supported by this study. In response to the statement *I enjoy learning French/German*, 23% of boys and 31% of girls agreed, while 28% of boys and 16% of girls registered their disagreement. In interviews, boys were more likely than girls to name modern languages as their least favourite subject. One Year 7 boy's response to the interview question, 'Where is French on your scale of subjects if your favourite is at the top and your least favourite at the bottom?' was typical of that of many of his male peers:

> *It's nearly at the bottom for me, just that far from the bottom. That little bit at the bottom is just for the games.*

The questionnaire results suggest, however, that modern languages lack appeal for both boys and girls. While the boys cited French most often as their least favourite subject, and German emerged as their third least favourite, the greatest number of girls claimed mathematics was their least favourite subject, with French in second place.

The findings would seem to support, to some extent, the conclusions drawn by other studies that pupils' attitudes to foreign languages are age-related. Figure 1 shows percentages derived from a questionnaire completed by 210 Year 7 pupils at the beginning of their first language lesson. The number of positive responses may reasonably be judged to be somewhat inflated as a result of pupils wishing to make a positive impression on their teachers in the first lesson, but the figures suggest that later differences in boys' and girls' attitudes may be rooted in these differential preconceptions of learning languages.

Figure 2, showing boys' responses by year group to the questionnaire statement 'I enjoy learning French/German', suggests a deterioration in boys' attitudes to foreign languages as they grow older. Such figures suggest that boys' attitudes may not deteriorate until after Year 9, although an increasing uncertainty in Year 9 is suggested by the greatest number of *It's OK* votes. Such statistics should, however, be viewed with caution, given that the cohorts are neither equal in number nor constitute representative, parallel samples.

Similar uncertainty is reflected in the Year 9 girls' responses, while the percentage of positive responses from each year group suggests that girls' attitudes to modern languages are more favourable than boys' throughout school. The disparity between boys' and girls' attitudes is most evident in Year 11 and would seem to undermine the theory that boys' increased negativity at this stage is a common phenomenon among all pupils, regardless of sex, and symptomatic of exam pressure, rather than a reaction to the subject itself.

In interviews a number of pupils described enjoying languages more in Years 7, 8 and 9 than in Years 10 and 11 when, ostensibly, the novelty value had diminished, topics already worked through were being revisited and the level of difficulty had increased.

Are you looking forward to learning languages?
The responses of Year 7 pupils in their first modern languages lesson in secondary school

	n	YES	NOT SURE	NO
BOYS	96	73%	22%	5%
GIRLS	114	89%	10%	1%
BOYS + GIRLS	210	81%	16%	3%

Figure 1

I enjoy learning French/German
The responses of boys by year group
(n=382)

YEAR GROUP	n	YES	IT'S OK	NO
7	63	26%	44%	31%
8	117	26%	48%	26%
9	85	28%	57%	15%
11	117	14%	46%	39%

Figure 2

Contact with native speakers

In interviews, a number of pupils attributed their high motivation in language learning to having had the opportunity to communicate with native speakers on exchanges, trips or family holidays. The suggestion that motivation may be dependent on the provision of such opportunities could, of course, have serious implications for the large number of pupils, often from low-income homes, who are denied the experience of travel abroad; of the 799 pupils who completed the questionnaire, 53% of pupils had never visited a country where the foreign language was spoken. Pupils' experiences of travel abroad varied widely from school to school: in the school with the most affluent catchment area, 67% of pupils had been to a target language country more than once, while in an inner-city school, a comparable percentage – 73% – had never had this opportunity.

The lack of opportunities for use of the language in a real context might well be anticipated to have an adverse effect on pupils' attitudes to languages. The consequences might be considered to be particularly serious for boys if, as some researchers have suggested (e.g. Gardner, 1985), they are primarily 'instrumentally' motivated by opportunities to apply newly-acquired knowledge in real-life contexts. A comparison of the two schools mentioned above reveals that there is something of a difference in pupils' attitudes, suggesting a positive correlation with visits abroad. Of those pupils who had the most opportunities to use the language abroad, 33% claimed to enjoy learning languages. Of those who had the fewest opportunities, 27% of pupils expressed their enjoyment.

The possibility that this difference may well be attributable to other factors should not be ignored. It would seem, however, that if boys are denied this opportunity, their attitudes are more likely to be negative. While 24% of boys who had been abroad more than once claimed that they did not enjoy languages, 30% of boys who had never been abroad expressed their dislike. This latter figure invites an interesting comparison with girls who had never been abroad; 17% of them expressed their dislike, suggesting that contact with native speakers abroad may well be perceived to be of greater importance by boys than girls.

Pupils' evaluation of their ability

This study seems to confirm the conclusions of other research that boys display a general tendency to rate their own academic ability highly, while girls display more modesty (O'Brien, 1985: 36–40; Batters, 1988: 128; Graham, 1994: 15). In interviews, boys were often far less inhibited than girls in rating their ability:

> *I prefer French because I'm very good at it. I'm a natural at it.* (Year 8)

Boys did not, on the whole, rate their ability as superior to girls', a finding which supports Batters' conclusion (Batters, 1988: 134). Both in interviews and in response to the questionnaire, the overwhelming majority – 74% of boys and 80% of girls – claimed that there was no difference in boys' and girls' abilities in languages.

In interviews a number of boys did, however, demonstrate an awareness of girls' alleged academic superiority:

> *Mr. X says that girls get better marks, but I don't think there's any difference.* (Year 7)

> *When I was watching the news it was saying that girls are proving to be more clever than boys in all subjects.* (Year 8)

It is, it seems, only in the later years of schooling that boys are more likely to accept that girls are academically more successful. This realisation could well generate demotivation among boys and is, according to one Year 10 boy, a strong argument for segregation:

> ... *'Cos when you've got girls in the room, and you hear their results,compared with the boys', you might feel a bit low. It makes you feel better with boys, who are on average the same.*

Pupils' perceptions of the importance and relevance of language learning

Pupils' perceptions of the relevance of language learning is generally acknowledged by researchers to be a highly important factor in creating extrinsic motivation to do well in the subject (Powell, 1986; Graham & Rees, 1995; Clark & Millard, 1998). Graham and Rees's conclusion (1995: 18) that this is more important for instrumentally motivated boys would seem to be corroborated by this study. The 60 boys in the three single-sex groups who completed another questionnaire in June 1998 attributed more importance to this than their female counterparts: 67% rated as 'important' '*knowing that you'll use your French in the future*', compared with 49% of the girls. While girls may more readily accept the necessity of learning a language (Clark & Trafford, 1996: 42), and often seem happy to enjoy it without assessing its future applications, boys' attitudes are often determined by an awareness of the usefulness of language learning:

> *Knowing you'll use your French in the future [is important]. I ain't never going to use it, so there's no point in learning.* (Year 9 boy)

The disparity between boys' and girls' evaluation of the usefulness of languages is most evident in Year 11: 29% of boys reject the idea that learning a language is useful, compared with 12% of girls. Further evidence of this development is revealed in pupils' responses to '*French/German is a waste of time*': 30% of boys in Year 11 agree with this highly negative statement, compared with only 9% of the girls. It is, of course, significant that this disparity, and boys' readiness to subscribe to what amounts to a statement of the futility of learning a language, is most evident in the year when pupils sit their GCSE examinations.

In interviews pupils often claimed that languages were not as important as other subjects:

> (Boys, Year 8)
>
> S: *...French probably wouldn't get you a job, but if you're good at maths and English...*
>
> C: *Maths and English, that's more like general knowledge, isn't it?*
>
> M: *Science...those are the sorts of things you've got to know. I don't like them, but I have to do them, that's my view.*

Considerable hesitation was shown by many pupils when asked in interviews if they would use their languages in the future. Pupils' perceptions of language use, for holidays and work, were restricted to opportunities abroad; none of the pupils interviewed referred to the possibility of using a foreign language in the UK, a misconception which is perhaps endorsed by the predominance of the overseas scenario in the GCSE examination. The following response to the interview question, 'Do you think you will use your French in the future?' is typical of many:

> Boys (Year 7)
>
> R: *Some people might want to go on holiday, but some people don't like the French, so they won't go over.*
>
> D: *It'd be pretty useful if you like going to France.*
>
> C: *It depends. Me and S, like, we're going on the French exchange, so it'll help us there, won't it? So sometimes it can come in useful.*

Higher ability pupils are, it seems, more likely to perceive the relevance of languages to their careers. In response to the 1997 questionnaire, 40% of pupils of lower ability claimed that they would not use French or German when they left school, compared with 19% of higher ability pupils. In interviews, the greatest awareness of the vocational relevance of learning languages was demonstrated by boys and girls who attended the school with the most affluent catchment area:

(Girls, Year 9):

V: *... if you work on an aeroplane as an air hostess you need to know different languages, and travel agents. If you got transferred to a different country as well.*

A: *Or if you're an engineer or a chemist ...*

R: *Or a French and German teacher.*

(Boy, Year 9):

... European languages would be [useful] because now it's all Europe and everything, so, like your job, you're going to be moving around Europe a lot. It would be handy to know different European language ... My Dad works in Holland ...

67% of the pupil respondents from this school had been more than once to a country where the foreign language was spoken. This suggests that the experience of travel abroad, which is invariably linked to pupils' socio-economic background, is perhaps one of the most important of those variables considered which determine pupils' perceptions of the relevance of languages. This has significant implications for the role of school visits and exchanges and the associated pedagogy of an exchange.

Pupils' perceptions of modern languages as a girls' subject

It is commonly assumed that much male disinterest in modern languages can be attributed to the subject's alleged feminine image. A number of studies have revealed, however, that pupils generally demonstrate a reluctance to see the subject as sex-specific (Powell & Littlewood, 1983: 38; O'Brien, 1985: 40; Weinrich Haste, 1986 in Thomas, 1990: 34; Lee, Buckland & Shaw, 1998: 46). Interview and questionnaire responses in this study seem to confirm this finding; 95% of all pupils claimed in the questionnaire that modern languages are equally important for boys and girls, and none of the pupils interviewed perceived the subject to be more appropriate for one sex than the other. The apparent indignation with which interview questions referring to this were often received, however, along with the sometimes exceptionally vehement dismissal of the idea, suggested that pupils' awareness of 'political correctness' may well have influenced their responses, an interpretation shared by Lee, Buckland and Shaw in their account of interviews with Year 9 pupils (1998: 46).

Conclusions

That boys' and girls' attitudes towards modern languages are seemingly most disparate in Year 11 may be interpreted both as a reflection and cause of the disparity in their GCSE performance in the subject in the same year. While it seems that neither boys nor girls perceive languages as particularly enjoyable, boys' dislike of the subject seems to increase at a much faster rate than girls'. This may be exacerbated by pupils' experience of the increased difficulty of the subject at Key Stage 4 and by the lack of male appreciation of the relevance of languages. Pupils' awareness of the applications of languages is often limited to travel and tourism. The evidence of this study suggests both that pupils who travel abroad rate languages more highly and that this variable is likely to have a greater effect on boys' motivation than girls'. The part played by socio-economic factors, such as family income, in creating this opportunity should not be ignored.

The suggestion that boys do not succeed in language learning because they see it as a 'girls' subject' was thrown into question by pupils' responses in this study which should, perhaps, be heeded by those tempted to depict the subject in this way. The pupils' unequivocal dismissal of the notion that languages are more important for girls contrasts, however, with a number of their teachers' views, many of whom suspected that girls were more likely to see the subject as more important for them. This discrepancy, where it exists, may have serious implications for boys' motivation; teachers who subscribe to this notion may, like the teacher described in Sunderland's study (1998), be tempted to have higher expectations of their female pupils, and to gear their teaching towards them.

There are strong grounds for suggesting that success in modern languages is more heavily dependent on pupil motivation than in other subjects. In a subject that is so heavily interpersonal, as opposed to being led by an impersonal, factual content, pupils must be ready to face the challenge of learning by linguistic regression – using simple, childish language – to empathise with speakers of other languages and to internalise foreign behaviours. Motivating equally boys and girls from different backgrounds, and with varying interests and personalities, is clearly one of the greatest challenges for modern languages teachers.

Amanda Barton's findings suggest that neither boys nor girls particularly enjoy languages but that boys' dislike seems to increase at a faster rate than that of girls. In a classroom teaching context, which includes both boys and girls, Dörnyei's Group specific motivational components need to be acknowledged:

- given that pupils (within this sample) who travel abroad, rate languages more highly – increase the group's goal-orientedness; develop group cohesion and enhance intermember relations by working towards the exchange visit;
- given that language learning is a heavily interpersonal experience – encourage each student to be the best that she or he can be: avoid comparison with other students; make evaluations private rather than public; seek pupils' opinions;
- given that pupils perceive languages as difficult – minimise the detrimental effect of evaluation on instrinsic motivation

Bibliography

Aplin, R 'Why do Pupils Opt out of Foreign Language Courses? A Pilot Study' in *Educational Studies*, Vol. 17, No. 1: 3–13 (1991)

Batters, J *Pupil and Teacher Perceptions of Foreign Language Learning and Teaching* (unpublished PhD thesis, University of Bath, 1988)

Burstall, C et al *Primary French in the Balance* (NFER, 1974)

Clark, A and E Millard (eds.) *Gender in the Secondary Curriculum* (Routledge, 1998)

Clark, A and J Trafford 'Return to gender: boys' and girls' attitudes and achievements' in *Language Learning Journal,* 14: 40–49 (1996)

Gardner, R C *Social Psychology and Second Language Learning* (Arnold, 1985)

Graham, J *Gender Differences and GCSE results* (Keele University, 1994)

Graham, S and F Rees 'Gender differences in language learning: the question of control' in *Language Learning Journal,* 11: 18–19 (1995)

HMI *Boys and modern languages* (DES, 1985)

Lee, J, Buckland, D and G Shaw *The Invisible Child* (CILT, 1998)

Loulidi, R 'Is language learning really a female business?' in *Language Learning Journal*, 1: 40–43 (1990)

O'Brien, J *The Modern Language Image* (unpublished M.Ed. dissertation, University of Nottingham, 1985)

Powell, R and P Littlewood 'Why choose French? Boys' and Girls' Attitudes at the Option Stage' in *British Journal of Language Teaching* Vol. 21, No. 1: 36–39, 44 (1983)

Powell, R *Towards a Better Understanding of the Foreign Language Education of Boys and Girls in Comprehensive Schools* (unpublished PhD thesis, University of Bath, 1986)

Sunderland, J 'Girls being quiet: a problem for foreign language classrooms?' in *Language Teaching Research*, Vol. 2, No. 1: 48–82 (1998)

Thomas, K *Gender and Subject in Higher Education* (SRHE & Open University, 1990)

Chapter 3

What turns them on and what turns them off?

Factors influencing pupils' decisions whether or not to take foreign a language to A level and beyond

Keith Marshall

More pupils are taking GCSE modern languages. A decreasing number are taking their language study beyond to A level. Why is this so? What can be done about it? Keith Marshall provides interesting data which, when related to Dörnyei's motivational framework and Gardner's socio-educational model, may point a way forward.

Introduction

The last few years have seen a drop in the number of pupils taking languages at A level and in degrees courses. During the early 1990s, the great increase in the numbers at GCSE and university-wide programmes so engaged our attention and energies, that the decline in specialist learning beyond KS4 attracted less attention than it deserved. However, the persistence of the downward trend is impossible to ignore. Hopes that it might only be a temporary blip, or that increases in Spanish would compensate for decreases in French and German, appear increasingly unrealistic.

Entries for A level languages in the UK

	1992	*1997*	*% change*
French	31,261	25,881	-17.2%
German	11,338	10,440	-7.9%
Spanish	4,720	5,606	+18.8%
TOTAL	**47,319**	**41,927**	**-11.4%**

QCA data

Admissions to HE courses in the UK

	1990	*1997*	*% change*
Single French	1, 183	990	-16.3%
Single German	528	354	-33%
Single Spanish	300	243	-22.3%
All HE courses	**191,022**	**336,338**	**+76.1%**

UCAS data

Admissions to Joint Honours

	1995	*1997*	*% change*
Languages joint degrees	2,754	2,696	-2.1%
Joint languages(s) with a non-language subject	10,114	10,586	+4.7%
All HE courses	**290,596**	**336,338**	**+15.7%**

UCAS data

These data make for worrying reading. Single honours languages courses appear to be in precipitous decline. Is this a reflection of students reluctant to put all their eggs in one foreign language basket, fearing that this may limit career choice? This may be supported by the data relating to Joint Honours. While numbers taking Joint Honours in languages are declining, the rate is by no means as disturbing as that for single honours. A language plus another non-language subject, for which numbers are on the increase, may be seen as keeping career doors open rather wider.

Survey: scope and purpose

The present survey represents a provisional attempt to throw light on this issue. One hundred and seventy-nine Year 12 pupils from eight schools and colleges in the state and private sector were asked, during the Autumn Term of 1998–9, about:

- their attitudes to languages learning;
- the general thinking behind their choice of A levels;
- their reasons for choosing whether or not to do languages in particular;
- their plans, if any, for learning languages at university.

All had Grades A*, A or B in language GCSEs and were therefore capable of going on to A level. 42 had opted to do at least one A level language, 137 had opted not to.

The enquiry tool was a questionnaire with 174 questions. Respondents were presented with statements and asked to tick boxes indicating how far they agreed with each statement. The range of options was:

Agree strongly	Agree	Neither agree nor disagree	Disagree	Disagree strongly

The analysis presented here examines:

- the evidence from all respondents (linguists and non-linguists) regarding
  - attitudes to language learning
  - general considerations in choice of A levels;
- the opinions, motives and aspirations of
  - those doing an A level language
  - those not doing an A level language.

General attitudes to languages of all respondents (linguists and non-linguists): shared views and contrasts

As a background, we asked all 179 how they felt about languages generally. We wanted to find out:

- what their school experience of languages had been to date;
- whether those around them affected their attitudes to language learning;
- their perception of how useful languages might be in the world of work.

Predictably, the linguists were more enthusiastic than the non-linguists about the enjoyment of language learning (88% to 41%), interest in other cultures (71% to 63%) and speaking more than one other language (74% to 54%). However, only 11% of the non-linguists professed no interest whatever in learning more than one other language, and only 18% said they would have dropped languages earlier if allowed to do so (indeed 57% said they would not have done so). The suggestion that you can always get by with English, rejected by 57% of linguists, was supported by only 23% of the non-linguists. And there was a common enthusiasm (81%) among the 179 respondents (both linguists and non-linguists) for visiting other countries and people.

A general satisfaction emerged among linguists and non-linguists alike regarding the experience of language learning in schools, 74% of linguists and 63% of the others agreeing or agreeing strongly that they were well taught at GCSE. Their intellectual climate, as determined by the attitudes to Europe of the media, political parties and employers, was a negative force, particularly for the non-linguist. 43% of linguists and 37 % of non-linguists said they had received little or no encouragement from politicians, for example. In the home, only 22% of the non-linguists and 43% of linguists had found encouragement. The enthusiasm for their subject among linguists is predictable, but even among the non-linguists there are encouraging signs of a reservoir of positive feeling. 69% of them said they had no problem with languages, they simply preferred other subjects; and only 36% of them said they would never consider doing an A level language.

LANGUAGES AND EMPLOYMENT

Very few of the non-linguists (7%) dismissed languages as having no practical application and, although 36 % of them believed a GCSE language was enough for their career needs, 31% believed that an A level language would help their career prospects. Among all 179 respondents there was widespread ignorance about the employability of language graduates compared to graduates in other disciplines:

- only 24% knew that unemployment was lower among language graduates than computing graduates;
- only 21% knew that unemployment was lower among language graduates than physical sciences graduates;
- only 16% knew that unemployment was lower among language graduates than business studies graduates.

The table below gives the actual figures for 1997.

UNEMPLOYMENT RATES AMONG UK GRADUATES (1997)

French	3.5%
German	5.6%
All modern languages	5.7%
Computing	6.4%
Physical Sciences	7.1%
Business Studies/Management	7.2%

Higher Education Statistics Agency data

Overall considerations in pupils' choice of A levels: linguists and non-linguists

To provide a fuller background picture, we asked all 179 pupils to tell us about their general reasons for choosing A level subjects. The non-linguists demonstrated a slightly sharper awareness of the positive reasons which had informed their choices. So, whereas 76% of linguists said they chose the subjects they liked best, this was the case for 85% of the non-linguists; while 34% of linguists went for the most challenging subjects, 40% of the non-linguists did so. Non-linguists also showed a clearer long-term perspective: 38% told us their A level choices were dictated by their intended university course, as against only 15% of linguists.

Teachers often quote the difficulty of A level language learning as a reason why many pupils opt out after GCSE (see Marshall in: Shaw (ed), *Aiming High 2*, CILT, 2000). Given that view, it is surprising that 80% of our 179 respondents said they did not believe that it was more difficult to get good grades in modern languages than in other subjects. And the pupils are supported by the fact that, in 1997, 41.6% of A level candidates in French, 43.7% in German and 47.3 % in Spanish got As or Bs, as against an average of 35.2% across all subjects (QCA, 1999). On the issue of admission to university courses, in contrast, most of our 179 respondents were not well informed: only 5% understood that it was not more difficult to get into university to study languages, since there are so many empty places in university language departments as a result of falling applications (see Shaw above, Introduction).

Pupils who do opt for an A level language: positive motives, the wider A level context and long-term aspirations

To elucidate the motivation of the linguists, we:

- investigated the prevalent reasons for their language choice;
- put their choice into the additional context of
  - their other A levels
  - their university ambitions.

The language choice

For linguistists, personal development and life-style aspirations emerge as most influential. Top of the list is travel/visiting other countries and people, cited by 81%. The desire to study abroad comes close behind, similarly mentioned by 73%. Exactly what they can study is rather less important. So studying foreign cultures (50%), contemporary issues (42%), real life problems (36%), the past

(37%), foreign literatures (35%) attract middling numbers of these A level linguists. On the other hand, another 36% express no interest whatever in the prospect of studying foreign literature. The notion that A levels are also about more general intellectual development is widely appreciated. 43% expect the A level experience to develop their critical abilities and to enable them to think logically. So far as the ease of language learning is concerned, 36% said it was a positive factor for them, but this is counterbalanced by 26% who do not find languages easy, even if they are doing them for A level.

Materialistic motives, though not top of the list, had also been considered. Vocational language skills were, of course, the most frequently mentioned (66%), but many (47%) expected that they would acquire other vocational skills. A majority (60%) aspired to work abroad. Most (54%) were sure that the A level language would help them to find a job more easily, with almost half (45%) confident that a well-paid career awaited them and only 9% at all doubtful about their financial prospects. 23% were interested in being translators, but only 10% showed a moderate interest in teaching. Some 15% of language graduates eventually go into teaching, and less than 2% become translators.

The majority of our sixth form linguists had taken the advice of others before selecting their A levels. Most influential of all were parents, 58% of whom exercised a positive influence and only 20% a negative one. Other advisers included teachers (54% positive and 15% negative) and careers advisers (49% positive and 22% negative). So far as the status of languages in the schools was concerned, 31% thought languages were a priority in their school, while, more worryingly, 37% thought they were not. More worryingly still, 38% thought languages were taught less well than other subjects in their school. Nonetheless, there was a demand for more opportunities to do languages at A level. While 54% of these linguists said there was no room on their current timetable, 30% would have liked, ideally, to do another A level language, 9% even wanting to do two more. This indicates a constraint in the present A level system which the new A/AS exams may alleviate.

Linguists' other A levels

By asking the A level linguists about their motives for choosing their other subjects, we wanted to see how far they differed from and how far they matched the thinking behind the language choice. Significantly, career and vocational considerations, of secondary importance in the language choice, were predominant in the other subjects. 76% identified getting a job more easily as the major consideration in choosing these other subjects. 66% mentioned specifically that the other subjects would help them enter their intended profession and 65% hoped these subjects would lead to a well-paid career. But they were also looking to these subjects (more than to the languages) to provide them with certain interesting learning experiences, such as practical projects, field trips and hands-on experiments. They expected them to help develop their capacity for logical thought (66%) and their critical abilities (66%), at the same time as allowing them to study real-life issues (59%).

While the majority of the 42 linguists said they had not yet decided what to study at university, seventeen of them told us they did not intend to continue with languages there. Nine wanted to specialise in one or more of their other A level subjects, and ten believed that degrees in those subjects would improve their job prospects, although only two said they thought the career prospects for linguists were not good. There were some expressions of anxiety among this small group about having to study literature, about the prospect of spending a year abroad and about the cost of four-year degrees.

Lack of interest in progressing from A level to a university language degree is very much in line with trends since 1992/3, but the numbers involved in this small section of the survey are too small for us to draw definite conclusions both as regards the motives of sixth formers and possible counter-measures. On the bright side, at that early stage in Year 12, there was time to win back the doubters and influence the decisions of the 60% of linguists who had not yet made up their minds what to do at university, before they all filled in UCAS forms at the beginning of Year 13.

Pupils who choose not to do an A level language: non-linguists, but not anti-linguists

The most interesting section of our respondents, from the point of view of those of us who wish to see more language expertise in school leavers, are the ones who, though they had achieved grade A*, A or B at GCSE, had chosen not to do a language A level. Their responses suggested that these non-linguists were not anti-linguists.

MOSTLY TURN-OFFS, BUT ...

Coming at their motivation from the point of view of what A level languages might **not** enable them to do, we explored areas relating to:

- the experience of language learning;
- general intellectual development;
- skills acquisition;
- the content and learning methods of the course;
- getting a job and the nature of the job.

Hardly surprisingly, significant numbers agreed or agreed strongly that languages would not provide them with opportunities to engage in experiments (41%), practical projects (36%) and develop numeracy skills (34%). Slightly lower numbers felt that languages would not enable them to learn something practical (27%), learn to think logically (25%), study real-life issues (21%). And they drop further in relation to getting out of the classroom on field trips, developing their critical abilities and studying the past (all 18%), studying literature (15%) and acquiring vocational skills (13%).

There is a big disincentive for the 39% who told us that A level languages would not enable them to enter their intended profession, but the numbers expressing serious, wide-ranging doubts about the inadequacies of languages in relation to career prospects were, on the whole, low. Some believed languages would not help them get a hands-on practical job (26%), or enter a well-paid career (19%), or simply get a job more easily (14%). But the remarkable thing is that, in relation to many of these considerations – practical projects, learning to think logically, studying real-life issues, getting a practical job, acquiring vocational skills, studying literature and the past – an even larger proportion of the non-linguists told us that these potential inadequacies had not played a part in their decision not to do an A level language.

On the experience of language learning and personal perceptions of languages, there is a similar pattern. Significant numbers agree or agree strongly that they did not do languages because they are boring (31%), incomprehensible (21%), impractical (20%), too abstract (12%) or would oblige them to study grammar (31%) or literature (26%). But virtually none dismissed languages as a waste of time (8%) or shallow (7%). Once again, remarkably, substantially larger numbers asserted that these negative perceptions of languages and of the language learning experience had nothing to do with their decision not to study a language at A level.

There is a suspicion that external advice plays a part in turning young people away from languages. Not surprisingly, some (20%) say they got on better with the teachers of their chosen A level subjects and others (19%) reckoned the subjects they had chosen were better taught at GCSE than languages. Nonetheless, negative advice from careers advisers (12%), teachers (9%) and parents (11%) had a decisive influence in a very small number of cases. On the contrary, 61% said of their careers advisers and 65% of both their parents and teachers that they did not put them off languages.

Conclusion: possibilities for increasing language take-up at A level and university

The findings of this survey are tentative in that they are based on a sample, sections of which are small. A fuller, more subtle picture should be provided by a much larger data-set now being drawn from some 100 schools. Despite its size, however, this data-set has allowed us to identify a number of points regarding the motivation of pupils passing from the compulsory language regime of Key Stage 4 to the relative freedom of choice of the sixth form. To reverse the decline in specialist language learning in sixth forms/FE colleges and at universities, we must target the two different groups, discussed in this investigation:

- those who drop languages after Year 11;
- those who do an A level language, but do not intend to go further.

While some of the first group are determined non-linguists, the remainder include a substantial minority who enjoy studying languages, can see career advantages in taking them on to A level, but are prevented from doing so by the current system of three or four subject specialisation in the sixth form. 27 of those we questioned, who are not doing a language under the present system, said that, given the chance to do another A level, they would do a language. If they all had been able to do that, the number of A level language students across these eight schools would have increased by 50%. Clearly, adding on another A level to the present sixth form would not be possible, but the new Curriculum 2000 allowing pupils to do more subjects at A/AS levels in Years 12 and 13 should open up the way for more frustrated linguists to develop their talent.

Other factors discouraging a significant number of potential linguists in both groups are the widespread ignorance and misunderstanding, revealed in the survey, about the relative employability of language graduates. While not as fundamental perhaps as intrinsic factors in the complex psychology of learning motivation, the fact that among language specialists the rate of unemployment is lower than among all other graduates could tip the balance in a student's choice of courses.

The second group, those who abandon languages after A level, require the combined efforts of the language staff in sixth forms/FE colleges and universities. By collaborating to create a continuity between the two institutional levels, showing that languages are exciting, the course combinations infinitely variable and the outcomes rewarding, we can help ensure that no students abandon languages out of ignorance of what languages can do for them.

Marshall's data relate closely to Dörnyei's Learning Situation Level and Gardner's Language Acquisition Context. If foreign language uptake is to improve, then an A level structure has to be created within which those students wishing to take a foreign language are encouraged rather than restricted, as they are by the current structure. Will post-16 reform lead to more students taking foreign languages at AS? This would be a good thing. How many will then make the transition from AS to A level? Will the completion of the AS course mark the end of the school foreign language learning experience?

Teachers may also be advised to take account of the Teacher-specific motivational components aspect of Dörnyei's framework and invest more time in promoting the usefulness and relevance of foreign languages in the world of work. Marshall refers to the students' perceptions of the employability of foreign languages graduates which may relate to Gardner's social milieu, in that a milieu needs to be created which engenders a more positive view of foreign language learning and the relevance of foreign language competence.

Interesting links can also be made between other levels of Dörnyei's framework and Marshall's findings which identify areas within which strategies should be implemented to improve the totality of the foreign language learning experience:

Dörnyei's level	**Marshall's findings**
Learning situation level	Enjoyment of foreign language learning
	Relevance of the syllabus (literature dimension?)
Language level	Interest in other cultures
	Employment opportunities
Learner level (Gardner's social milieu)	Encouragement from home
	Hands-on/practical dimension/other skills

Chapter 4

Able pupils in modern foreign languages

David Stork

David Stork describes and critically analyses a problem common to many local authorities: under-achievement. Although he focuses on the more able pupils, the underlying theme is the challenge of enhancing low self-esteem. The links between the solutions implemented and Dörnyei's learner-situation and learner levels are manifold.

The context

Modern foreign languages represented an area of concern in the East Riding of Yorkshire: underachievement, especially among the more able, pupils' negative perception of their own ability and low levels of confidence. It was felt that something had to be done to ameliorate this situation. If levels of achievement were improved among the more able, then this might well have a backwash effect on pupils further down the achievement scale. A project was therefore funded to test the hypothesis that:

> *... the attainment of all pupils can be enhanced if the attainment of the highest achievers is improved.*

Project aims:

- to identify a cohort of approximately 36 pupils of high linguistic ability within seven project schools;
- to identify the characteristics and preferred teaching and learning styles of upper ability pupils; and

- to establish the needs of these pupils in terms of lexical and grammatical progression;
- to develop the use of value added techniques in measuring progression in modern foreign languages;
- to increase the number of A* pupils at GCSE by 2% per year, and the number of pupils at Level 6 by 7.5% per year over the next three years;
- to raise attainment in modern foreign languages.

The project schools

The seven schools participating in the first phase of the project chose to do so; in this respect, therefore, the sample is not a selected one. By virtue of its range, however, it does represent a fair cross-section of the schools in this region, both in terms of the geographical location (rural, large town, small town, edge of large conurbation), and in terms of the range of ability as defined by cognitive ability testing. They also contain the smallest and the largest of the East Riding's secondary schools, a school in a town in receipt of a European Social Regeneration Grant, and a single-sex girls' school.

Identifying the able pupil

It was felt that the provision of subject-specific criteria for MFL was an essential part of this project. Denton and Postlethwaite (1982) have carried out a great deal of research into the criteria for the identification of able pupils in a range of subjects. Their checklist for able pupils in MFL, slightly modified, forms the basis for that applied in each school involved in this project (see Table 1). A major difference is the addition of a category related to the use of vocabulary.

A maximum score of 50 points is available on the checklist. Individual class teachers were asked to allocate scores 1-5 to individual pupils in each category, basing these on their own observations and judgements. In the interest of consistency, exemplar statements or categories were included. Schools were asked to identify the teacher for each set of returns, so that anomalous results could be checked. It was not intended that there should be a score for each statement, simply a single score in each line.

The schools submitted their results to the Research, Statistics and Quality Assurance Team in the East Riding of Yorkshire LEA to be processed and analysed against other indicators available such as Key Stage 2 results and Cognitive Ability Test (CAT) scores.

Table 1: Classroom performance in MFL: the checklist used in this project

Characteristic (with examples of how the characteristic may be demonstrated)	*Excellent (5)*	*Very Good (4)*	*Average (3)*	*Below Average (2)*	*Poor (1)*
1. Attitude: (a) shows enthusiasm (b) shows an interest in the foreign culture					
2. Vocabulary: willing to experiment					
3. Oral/Aural skills: (a) able to articulate foreign sounds (b) able to discriminate between foreign sounds					
4. Oral response: alert oral response to questions in FL (may be better than written)					
5. Control over sound/symbol correspondence: pronunciation not perverted by the written form of the language					
6. Self-confidence: (a) not embarrassed by speaking FL (b) willing to try out foreign sounds					
7. Memory: shows clear evidence of good memory					
8. Mastery of English: (a) knowledgeable of essential grammar, e.g. part of speech (b) alert to nuances in own language					
9. Flexibility: (a) can accept and understand an entirely new set of rules and think within them (b) does not try to impose English style or syntax on FL sentences when writing compositions					
10. Ability to put the language together: (a) independently makes new connections out of isolated units of knowledge (b) makes creative use of FL structures					
Total score for column:					
Total overall score:					

The correlation between the classroom scores in MFL and the KS2 and CAT scores did not prove to be very high, as Table 2 shows. The results did, however, indicate an important factor in the motivation of the more able, which is a hierarchy of skills. The more able, as shown by standardised scores, demonstrate greater ability in certain areas of language learning. This of itself is not surprising. What is significant is that these areas are not necessarily those which are most frequently seen in lessons. Some apparently obvious indicators such as oral ability and self-confidence, which are more in the affective domain, are not necessarily indicators of ability. If able pupils are to be adequately challenged and therefore motivated in the modern foreign language classroom, it would seem from these figures that there is a need to ensure that the balance between the top five skills must be properly struck.

Table 2: Correlation results: MFL classroom performance to standardised scores

Question	av.cat score	KS2 test
flexibility	0.44	0.37
memory	0.43	0.38
mastery of English	0.42	0.37
sound/symbol correspondence	0.42	0.37
ability to put language together	0.41	0.33
oral/aural skills	0.38	0.39
vocabulary: willing to experiment	0.34	0.36
oral response	0.27	0.31
self-confidence	0.24	0.27
attitude and interest	0.17	0.2

Professional assessments and the role of the class teacher

The role of the class teacher in recognising potential through daily assessment of the pupil is without doubt of paramount importance. Assessment here does not necessarily include testing, either, but the broader definition of observation of performance and looking for the kinds of factors listed above. Having identified the able pupil, how can that ability be built upon, and the pupil suitably motivated?

Identification of teaching strategies for developing able linguists

HMI (DFE/HMI, 1992) identified a range of factors in class to support the development of able pupils, and the various factors identified can be seen in operation in the project schools:

- close attention to the needs of the individual pupil through differentiation of tasks;
- careful monitoring of individual progress;
- teachers with a deep understanding of their subjects;
- high expectations of what pupils can achieve;
- appropriate choice of resources;
- pupils being encouraged to think for themselves, to ask questions, to take some responsibility for their own learning and to contribute ideas;
- variation in pace, teaching style and classroom organisation;
- a stimulating learning environment.

In the light of this, the project schools have evolved the following three-point strategy:

1. The use of a general approach in class for accelerating progress

This consisted of a clear analysis of level descriptors and the involvement of pupils in understanding progression, and in the learning process. These students must become involved in their own learning in a way which allows them to know where they stand for instance in relation to the levels of the National Curriculum, and to help them to set realistic targets for themselves based on that knowledge. It must be made clear to them, however, how they are to achieve these targets. For the purposes of this project, an analysis of the level descriptors adapted from the optional task and test materials (Crossland and Horsfall, SCAA, 1995) has been used.

2. The pursuit of strategies in independent learning, involving the introduction of key skills, particularly ICT

In developing ways of motivating pupils of all abilities, ICT plays an important part. This was demonstrated in the survey, and is borne out in the practical experience of the schools in this project. To maintain and enhance this, it is intended to include pupils in the development of ICT strategies.

In their 1992 survey, HMI were critical of the way in which some extension tasks were set. These were seen often to lack appropriate learning objectives; the reward for finishing early or successfully was often more of the same. In differentiating for the able, therefore, it is important to ensure that they are set tasks which are meaningful and have learning objectives appropriate to their needs. The power of the *National Grid for Learning* in supporting this work should not be underestimated. In the East Riding, it will support our work in three ways:

(i) It will provide an opportunity for teachers to share materials which will be web-based and accessible to a defined group of people within a given learning community.

(ii) It will provide opportunities for a defined user-group of able pupils, who will be able to access certain resources or web-based discussions (web conferencing) via a local intranet. This could include a remote tutor who manages additional tasks or topics to which pupils can have access. These topics can be linked to local schemes of work and thereby provide differentiated activities at a higher level.

(iii) In the East Riding, as a follow-up to this project, pupils will have access to video-conferencing for face-to-face contact either with other able students locally or their European counterparts. This will reinforce other key skills: communication, working with others, improving own skills and performance.

3. The identification of suitable materials to support these strategies

In the first instance, it was felt that it would be necessary to create teaching materials for extension tasks, and indeed, some teachers in the project have done so. Interesting reading materials and several *textes louffoques*, out of the ordinary, amusing and stimulating, have been written. It is becoming ever more the case, however, that publishers are producing materials aimed at the higher levels.

The materials are not, however, the only way to create stimulation, and in some cases normal class exercises or homeworks can be employed to challenge the more able. This is particularly true of extended writing and speaking tasks, which often go hand-in-hand with creativity and imagination, or the use of ICT or video resources. The schools which have been most successful in stimulating able students make systematic use of extended tasks, for instance setting ICT-based tasks to be completed over a period of time using desk-top publishing. An important element of this is to break the topic-based approach of text-books, which are often better used as a support for the learning process than to provide the whole diet. The integration of work from earlier units of work into, for instance, an interview with a celebrity or a pen-friend letter is an essential part of the challenge and an important element of progress.

Conclusion

Three of the project schools, who have embraced the idea of involving pupils in the learning process, have seen their performance at Key Stage 3 improve considerably, as the pupils' own expectations rise. These schools discovered very quickly that the idea of monitoring a small number of pupils for the project was not appropriate; all pupils in a set could benefit from this approach. In this respect, the hypothesis of the project has been borne out: the attainment of all pupils **can** be enhanced if the attainment of the highest achievers is improved.

In the wider context of the other project schools, while improvement in results may have been less spectacular, awareness among teachers has been raised and able pupils are now very much on the agenda. In some ways, no project can seek a more important outcome than to stimulate interest for others to follow: during the course of the work of this project, five further schools have joined in. They will have an important part to play in future developments.

Why has the project succeeded in enhancing achievement?

At Dörnyei's **learning situation level:**

- a variety of media and materials have been made accessible;
- there is a greater match between difficulty of tasks and pupils' abilities;
- pupils' expectancy of task fulfilment has been enhanced by the transparency of assessment methods and marking criteria.

At Dörnyei's **learner level:**

- pupils' self-confidence has been developed;
- strategies have been developed to promote pupils' self-efficacy to achieve learning; goals and develop realistic expectations;
- pupils have been helped to see the link between effort and outcome.

As Stork points out, this is not about good teaching for more able pupils. It's about good teaching and learning for all pupils.

Bibliography:

Crossland D and P.Horsfall: *Optional tasks and tests,* (SCAA, 1995)

Denton C and K. Postlethwaite *The identification of more able pupils in comprehensive schools,* (Oxford, 1982)

DFE/HMI, *Education observed: The education of very able children in maintained schools* (HMSO, 1992)

Other useful publications

Eyre D, *School governors and more able children* (DfEE, 1995)

Oxford R.L. *Language learning strategies, what every teacher should know* (University of Alabama, 1989).

Parry and Stansfield (eds.), *Language aptitude reconsidered* (Centre for Applied Linguistics, New Jersey, 1990)

Pillette M, *Tips for busy language teachers : Stretching the more able at 14–16* (Collins, 1997)

Weeks A, *Your gifted pupils: meeting the needs of the exceptionally able* (New Educational Press, 1993)

Chapter 5

Turning things around

Interview with Susan Chamberlain, Viewforth High School and Steven Fawkes, Education Officer, BBC

This chapter consists of two interviews which tell the story of a modern languages department given new life. The first interview is with the head of department, Susan Chamberlain, who contextualises the problem she and her colleagues faced and how they tackled it. The second is with Steven Fawkes who had a key influence on the transformation of German at Viewforth; he provides an insight into his teaching methodology and the rationale behind it. The course specific motivational component aspect of Dörnyei's learning situation level is relevant to both interviews, but does not provide the complete picture.

Interview with Susan Chamberlain

Editor: Tell me about the situation you inherited when you joined Viewforth.

Susan: I was very worried about the place of German in the school. Only those students who did well in their first year of French were offered the chance to do German in S2. (i.e. in the second year of secondary school education; pupils at age 13) This meant that only six to twelve students chose to do German each year. These students also represented the total number of 'dual linguists' in any year group. Given these very small numbers, there was a real danger that school management would question the feasibility of German and remove it from the timetable. I did not want to be leading a modern languages department which offered one language only, i.e. French. What message would this be sending to our pupils about the value of foreign languages?

Editor: So how did you set about changing things?

Susan: We decided that, rather than limiting access to German to the more able, all students should be required to take French and German in S2. They would then be in a position to make an informed choice at the end of that year whether they wanted to take French or German or French and German in S3. We sent a letter to all parents of S2 students explaining our intention and the importance of foreign language competence (see Appendix, p74).

Editor: Did it work?

Susan: I am delighted to report that it did. The numbers taking German have seen a dramatic rise. In 1997/98 55 pupils at the end of S2 opted to take German and 23 French. The following year 83 chose German and 12 French. Never before in the school's history have the numbers taking German been so healthy.

Editor: This can't just be the result of changing access to German. Was there not more to it than this?

Susan: Of course. My colleagues and I committed ourselves to investing even more of our energy and enthusiasm to our teaching of German. This manifested itself in a number of ways:

- we adopted a new course book, *Projekt Deutsch* (OUP). The pupils love it. It's so bright and colourful. The pupils get a real feeling of making progress, they don't spend an entire unit on how to say 'Hello', as is the case with some other coursebooks. The workbook has also proven to be a very positive feature;
- we exploited the BBC video *Hallo aus Berlin* and Channel Four's *Willkommen;* these were a great success;

I have to make a special mention of the songs on *Hallo aus Berlin*. The students loved these. They made up their own lyrics and dance routines for the songs and had their performances recorded on video. The video was then sent to the BBC. This served as a wonderful motivator for the students. The extent of the students' motivation is reflected in one session in which more than 70 of them gave up their lunch-hour to perform their songs and routines. This was followed by all concerned being awarded departmental *Certificates of Achievement* in a school assembly.

In December 1998 we experienced a special highlight when Steven Fawkes, the BBC Education Officer, visited the school. The students weren't the only ones to be excited about this. My colleagues and I learned so much from talking to him about his teaching philosophy. We had a great day. Steven did a fantastic job. The local newspaper sent a reporter and took pictures. This did the status of German a power of good.

Editor: So what's the next step?

Susan: In the academic year 1999/2000 we will have the largest number ever continuing with German in S5. We are no longer so worried about German and now want to apply ourselves to the status of French. We have learnt so much from the German experience. It is just a matter of applying this to French.

Interview with Steven Fawkes

Steven Fawkes is an Education Officer at the BBC and spends some of his time visiting classes to see how they respond to new broadcast and multimedia resources. His work in this area is well known and, as confirmed by Susan's reaction above, highly rated. What could we learn from him about motivating foreign language learners? I asked him to reflect on the challenge of engaging pupils and stimulating their creative and linguistic work.

Editor: What do you regard as the most important influence on pupil motivation?

Steven: Whatever pupils' distinctive learning preferences and interpretations, they identify **the teacher** as the central feature of the motivation they are looking for.

> *I think teachers have to be ... basically ... good teachers and have to be themselves interested in the subject and make other people interested in what they're doing and use ... different ways of teaching and ... just basically ... get people interested in what they're doing ... If the teacher's enthusiastic you feel that it's fun. You don't feel it's work...*
> (Girl, 15)

> *It is the teacher's fault, that's what I think, because it is the teacher's job, that's what they're paid for, ... to get you interested and to teach the subject.*
> (Girl, 15)

The human elements of the teaching relationship are crucial. In order to create a motivating atmosphere, the teacher needs to feel ownership of the lesson content. So, even if there is a prescribed resource (such as a textbook) with, for example, shared assessment tasks to be carried out by all, there are bound to be different routes that individuals (teachers and learners) can take in order to get to the same position in preparation for such tasks. The place of knowing one's students, professional judgement and reflection is paramount in this respect.

Editor: So what does this mean for the individual teacher?

Steven: On my frequent visits to classrooms in order to pilot new resources or observe classes responding to them I have often noted the power of the teacher's sensitivity to particular issues and judicious choice from a range of elements:

- sensitivity to time;
- sensitivity to mood;

- sensitivity to response;
- choice of resource;
- choice of activity;
- choice of grouping.

Those learning activities which appear the most motivating may be inspired by the resource but are usually managed (and often created) by the teachers, using knowledge of the class, of the learning objectives and of all of the resources at their disposal.

The balance between the different elements of the classroom equation is often indefinable and may have many unpredictable elements in it; yet teachers in tune with their class and their subject use their expertise to move the lesson forward:

- spotting when an activity has (or has not) gone on long enough;
- spotting when the classroom dynamic is (or is not) right for a certain activity;
- spotting when the class is lost or is going through the motions;
- identifying which resource is getting the best response;
- discarding something which is not working and picking up something else;
- moving to and from individual work according to the feel of the class.

Teachers tend to articulate the view that it is learners of modest and lower ability who are more difficult to motivate, as they seem to have less of a long-term vision of their objectives. This is certainly not always the case.The expectation that more able learners are automatically focused on, and motivated by, longer-term aspirations does not match the foreign language teaching/learning reality.

Editor: Shortage of resources tends not to be such a big problem as it used to be. The challenge now is choosing the most appropriate resource. How should one set about doing this?

Steven: When researching the type of resources teachers value most highly for a recent television project, the following criteria came up regularly:

materials are useful when they:

- are short and focused;
- are not reliant on long-term memory;
- are subtly repetitious;
- have visual impact alongside the sound;
- are easy to access.

Consideration of these criteria (in order) raises some further interesting evaluative questions about my own practice:

- How does the concept of activities being **short and focused** match with the classroom teaching resources available?
- How does the suggestion of avoiding long-term memory work fit with the examination needs of the class?
- How can linguistic 'recycling' be integrated more into the teaching plan?
- What age-relevant strategies are useful for maintaining the visual input, and when is it necessary to reduce the amount of visual support offered?
- How dependent is the class on the continuous intervention and support of the teacher?

Resources which have the most enduring use in the classroom tend to be those which are highly flexible and which can be accessed by a wide ability- and age-range. Although frequently associated with a language topic, in order to be easily dropped into a scheme of teaching, they tend not to rely exclusively on what language has been covered previously, but instead on what the learners are involved in doing with a manageable amount of language, whether new or familiar.

These resources will each have different strengths, and may be:

- **print**: books, articles, realia, magazines, poems to present cultural information in appropriate contexts and formats;
- **audiotape**: songs, interviews, penpal texts to illustrate the sort of utterances which learners need to understand and to produce;
- **video**: documentaries, voxpops, presentations, animations to reassure the learners that they are able to understand the foreign language;
- **multimedia**: images, soundfiles, textfiles to intrigue the learner through interesting, age-relevant subject matter;
- **on-line**: drills, research activities, interactive games to encourage active involvement and enjoyment of the learning process;
- **human:** language assistants, exchange partners to provide the message that the foreign language is spoken by real people and for real purposes.

The resources may be completely authentic, specially edited (or rehearsed in terms of the human resources) or purpose-made, but they are under the editorial eye of the teacher, who selects them according to need, relevance and the potential they have for particular stimulation. The teacher may be more of an impresario than a performer, setting up the stage for the foreign language lesson.

> *My dear boy, forget about the motivation. Just say the lines and don't trip over the furniture.*

Noel Coward's admonition to an overly analytical young actor at rehearsal still pertains in part: it is important, with all of the internal and external requirements to which teachers have to adhere, to avoid obvious pitfalls and keep the basic tasks going; it is also important, however, for the teacher to consider where the energy for learning comes from, to understand her or his own motivation and philosophy in order, in turn, to convey it to the learners.

Two good teachers. Good materials. This doubtless helps with motivation but is not the whole story. Susan and Steven include a sociocultural component with the video and music (Dörnyei's language level). They provide attractive, authentic and accessible material and use a variety of media; they arouse and sustain curiosity and attention with the introduction of the unexpected and increase students' interest and involvement in tasks; they facilitate student satisfaction and celebrate success with the public presentation of Certificates of Achievement (Dörnyei's learning situation level). They match tasks to pupils' abilities/needs/ routes of learning; they show their enthusiasm and commitment to teaching and to teaching their subject (Dörnyei's teacher-specific motivational components).

Appendix

Letter sent to all parents explaining French and German for **all** S2.

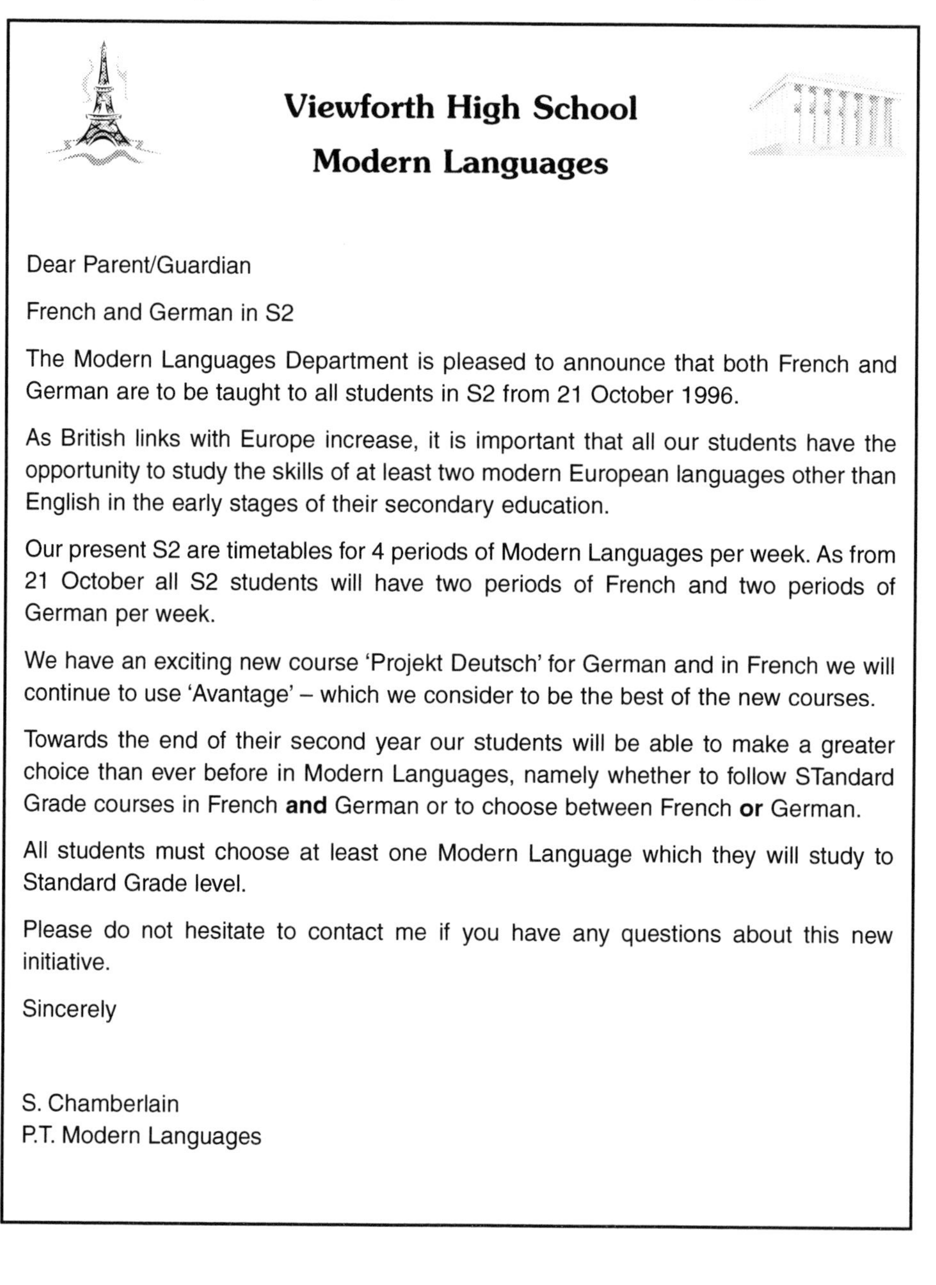

Viewforth High School
Modern Languages

Dear Parent/Guardian

French and German in S2

The Modern Languages Department is pleased to announce that both French and German are to be taught to all students in S2 from 21 October 1996.

As British links with Europe increase, it is important that all our students have the opportunity to study the skills of at least two modern European languages other than English in the early stages of their secondary education.

Our present S2 are timetables for 4 periods of Modern Languages per week. As from 21 October all S2 students will have two periods of French and two periods of German per week.

We have an exciting new course 'Projekt Deutsch' for German and in French we will continue to use 'Avantage' – which we consider to be the best of the new courses.

Towards the end of their second year our students will be able to make a greater choice than ever before in Modern Languages, namely whether to follow STandard Grade courses in French **and** German or to choose between French **or** German.

All students must choose at least one Modern Language which they will study to Standard Grade level.

Please do not hesitate to contact me if you have any questions about this new initiative.

Sincerely

S. Chamberlain
P.T. Modern Languages

Chapter 6

ICT makes it click

Jim McElwee

At the learning situation level Dörnyei recommends the implementation of varied media. Information and Communications Technology (ICT) is playing an increasingly common and significant role in the provision of this variety, contributing to a positive learning experience. Does it motivate just because it is perceived by pupils as a novelty in the foreign languages classroom? Jim McElwee illustrates how it can be exploited to take ICT beyond this.

Introduction

How does ICT motivate pupils? How can ICT stimulate pupils to consider the language they are learning and help them make the right connections? What impact that ICT have on the teacher's assessment of pupils' progress?

When we experience success with a particular activity as we teach a group, we tend to incorporate that activity into our general practice. Do we always probe as deeply as we should into the reasons why a strategy works? Is this not important if we are to understand better how our pupils make progress and the implications for how we might better assess their progress? I suggest that ICT can facilitate consideration of these issues. When pupils work individually, or in pairs in a computer suite, then, provided the activity has been planned carefully, the teacher has more freedom to assess pupils' progress and to observe how they learn. Moreover, there may well be a marked difference in motivation in other lessons where there is no element of ICT.

Not *plug and go*

Programs which stimulate aimless clicking are not the answer. The teacher needs to know what he or she wants the pupils to learn. Many applications help the student to learn new vocabulary, but if these building bricks are left unused to pile up in a corner of the brain, they will be ignored and forgotten. How do you judge the effectiveness of an activity? A superficial level of understanding can shroud the lack of real understanding in the area of focus. This can be illustrated by a group of teachers on an ICT course to learn the colours in Japanese from a CD-Rom. The teachers practised repeating words which matched the pictures of different coloured balls on the screen. They were all pleased with their pronunciation, and, when they proceeded to the test, found that they could match what they heard to the pictures. But there was a problem: what were they saying? Was it, *the ball is red*, or *a red ball*, or something else? They were not sure. One teacher remarked that she had not realised that we do the same thing to our pupils, often making assumptions that they understand what we are saying and what we are asking them to say. This is a problem which relates not only to ICT but to any target language-focused approach.

We should not, therefore, assume that following a sequence on a computer can lead to pupil learning; indeed, the opposite can sometimes be the case. For example, a group of Year 9 pupils were allowed to play a computer game which involved giving directions in order to arrive at a location on a map. Although pupils were able to provide the correct instructions, e.g. *tournez à droite, prenez la deuxième rue à gauche,* and complete the exercise correctly, many were unable to transfer their knowledge into a more active, open-ended situation. They had, therefore, **failed to make the connection**. Even though the pupils clearly enjoyed the activity, the learning outcomes were not what the teacher wanted. Again, although the illustration is ICT-specific, the problem is also a feature of the classroom where ICT is not a component. We need to be aware of the danger of being seduced by the medium and making the same mistakes when teaching in the target language with and without ICT support.

ICT provokes a need to know

Nevertheless, it is possible to achieve much by working with ICT that might not happen without it. Take for example some work done with a group of reluctant learners in their fourth year of learning German. Their attitude was not positive; indeed some pupils were so turned off that it was difficult to bring them back into a frame of mind where they would accept that they might achieve any success at all. Most pupils did, however, recognise that their teacher was working hard to help them to succeed.

The pupils had three 50-minute periods of German per week, as part of the school's policy of *languages for all* and followed the NEAB *Certificate of*

Achievement course which provided short-term goals which would be recognised by formal accreditation. The group had the use of multimedia laptops in the library once a week and these were installed with the old DOS version of *Fun with Texts*, which is a text-only program so there is no visual element. This was provided by worksheets made to accompany the units of the *Certificate of Achievement*, in this case the topic of *House and Home*. Pupils had to match the words and phrases in the file to the pictures on the sheets, by using the *Textsalad* option; then they tested themselves by using the *Copywrite* option. The next step was to move on to a more complicated file which described someone's house in a piece of continuous text.

At the end of the second session one of the boys asked, '*What is all this* der, dem *stuff then?*' All the boys around the table said, '*Yes, we wanted to ask that too.*' The theme for the next lesson had been identified. I prepared a grid which was divided into four columns: masculine, feminine, neuter and plural. Each of these contained ten pictures. At the left hand side of the sheet were verbs, with which the pupils were, or rather should have been, familiar. The top line showed the nominative form of the article with a dictionary symbol next to it. Next to the verbs was the accusative form. Rather in the manner of a chart for calculating the distance between towns, the pupils selected appropriate verbs and nouns to go with them, in order to make a correct sentence. Having reviewed the sentences and why they were correct and articulated a grammatical rule with which we felt comfortable, it was clear that the **connection** had been made.

We then looked at a list of the 40 German nouns relating to the topic. I asked the pupils to tick off the words they were sure they knew. To their pleasure (and mine), they knew all but four or five. It had never struck these pupils that they did, in fact, know so much. At the end of the lesson they said, '*That was great. Can we do something like this again next week?*'

Their reaction in the following lessons was just as positive. One of the girls informed me: '*For the first time I feel like I'm getting somewhere.*' The pupils now began to apply the rules, and used the word processor on their laptops to write a short passage about themselves and their family. Now they wanted to find things out for themselves and add to their work. Some produced pieces which moved them into *Foundation Level* of GCSE. We were able to ask them to consider the correct form of the article in the accusative case while they were writing. We were also delighted that these pupils, having enjoyed a modicum of success with their writing, now had a much more relaxed attitude about tackling their speaking assessment.

ICT shows up patterns

Working in pairs and groups often results in shared *aperçus*, which then help the learner to internalise a rule. It is important that the teacher should acknowledge and exploit pupils' discoveries and observations as he or she circulates round the class while the pupils work. If a list of items contains an obvious anomaly, it should provoke a reaction against the perceived lack of symmetry, but, as we know, this cannot be taken for granted. A computer screen can make all the difference. To illustrate this, I refer to the experience of a class using *Fun with Texts* to learn the spellings of different sandwiches in French. The pupils (a bottom set Year 8 group) had a sheet with the pictures of the sandwiches. They saw this list on the screen:

un sandwich au jambon

un sandwich au fromage

un sandwich aux tomates

un sandwich au pâté

un sandwich au poulet

un sandwich au thon

Two boys said, *Look sir, that one's got an x on the end.* The teacher suggested that they take a look at the pictures, and see if they could work out why:

Is it because there's more than one tomato?

Yes it is, would you like to explain it to everyone else?

The class then went on to discover some more rules, including the feminine form, *à la,* and then worked out, with a dictionary, how they would ask for sandwiches made of shrimps, lettuce, pork, salmon, crab and sardines. Ice cream desserts in the café then presented fewer problems. Pupils went on to look at these items in dialogues. They were able to write their own dialogues between a waiter and a customer with a high degree of accuracy.

The teacher was well aware that the pupils had seen these phrases in their written form on many occasions, yet only now did they **make a connection**. Again this prompted consideration of the question: '*What was it that finally made the penny drop?*'

ICT on the road to creativity

A frequent criticism of lessons at Key Stage 3 is the lack of opportunities provided for extensive reading and writing. This was a major consideration for the teacher of a Year 7 top set in a school in an Education Action Zone (EAZ). Pupils were positive but there were already signs of a fall in their application. The teacher decided to challenge them to produce an extended piece of writing which would incorporate elements of the language they had learned in the first two terms of the course. One element of the course book which she felt was lacking was a more explicit approach to grammar. The series of sessions in the computer room would ensure that this element would be stressed so that the class might acquire the knowledge needed to produce accurate text. As they learned more and more adjectives, it was necessary to help pupils learn the rules for agreement.

In the first lesson pupils were shown an overhead transparency (OHT) containing symbolic representations of the information they were going to use in their writing. Then they used a text and graphics manipulation program to match text to pictures. The pupils, working in pairs, studied the screen which had pictures of garments labelled, for example, *une chemise grise*. A click of the mouse scrambled all the nouns and adjectives, which the pupils then had to drag and drop beneath the appropriate pictures. It was deceptively easy and many pupils, especially the boys, gave the screen a cursory glance, before clicking. The teacher circulated, intervening gently, to suggest that they might like to start again. This time they took more care and started to consider the form of the adjectives.

After twenty minutes the teacher stopped the class and asked them to explain whether they had worked out any patterns. They were able to explain that the feminine nouns had an adjective ending in *-e,* and the masculine nouns did not. There were two plural words (*baskets* and *chaussettes*). Pupils were then able to see that plural words also added an *-s*, and recognised that this was a sort of pattern.

Work produced in the next lesson provided evidence that the pupils had retained their newly acquired knowledge and could see the pattern in a longer piece of text. The class was shown a letter written by a French girl. They had to read the letter and change the girl into a boy. All pupils worked assiduously on the task. They worked in pairs and discussed the changes that they needed to make. Each pair had a dictionary to help them find the correct masculine form of the adjectives. For example, the word *folle* occurred in the text, but few pupils failed to find the form *fou*.

In the third session pupils were asked to use the language they had been manipulating to write a letter about themselves. Their attitude was positive and all worked hard to complete the letter before the end of the session. The teacher's main observation was that the exercise had made the class read a longer passage carefully and reflectively, and that this had led to a general increase in competence in writing extensively.

Writing in reverse

A French teacher questioned the practice of colleagues in the English department of making pupils plan work on paper before copying it up on the word processor. She decided to reverse the process in her language lessons. Her pupils had completed a piece of written work on the computer, as a final activity in a series of exercises. As part of her feedback on progress she explained to them that they would have to write in pen in examinations, and that she would like to give them the opportunity to practise. They were asked to copy a passage similar to the one they had done on the computer, making changes only if they wished to. This resulted in a marked improvement in the general standard of performance and pupils were delighted to receive positive feedback.

Word order

Faced with pupils who had difficulty in grasping the concept of **time, manner and place** in German word order, a colleague decided to make a whole-class 'presentation' using a large computer screen. She cut clauses out of short sentences and pasted them into a longer sentence. Then she asked the pupils to do the same. Physically moving the text helped the pupils to understand the grammatical concept. One of the girls remarked that she only understood how the procedure worked by going through that process. The teacher used the same method to reinforce the change in word order after the word *weil*.

On-screen assessment

As we have already remarked, teachers can often respond more effectively to pupils' learning if they circulate while pupils are working on the computers. It is easier to identify common errors and misapprehensions and then to address these in the next lesson in the language classroom. It also helps identify areas for improvement. One teacher took the next logical step and started to mark pupils' work on the computer. When pupils had saved their work with an identifying code name, the teacher was able to access it, correct it by highlighting errors in bold or italics, and, where appropriate, add a comment at the foot of the document. In the next lesson, pupils were encouraged to re-read and correct the work, by amending the mistakes and converting them back to normal text. Had much the same process included use of the red pen, this would probably have had a demotivating effect. Doing it this way, however, appeared only to stimulate positively.

Conclusion

Much has been said and written about the power of ICT to motivate pupils to learn, but less has been said about **how** and **why** it does this. Reflective teachers try to note the point at which the penny drops and what it is that makes it drop. When computer-based activities are well constructed and planning includes assessment and progression, teachers and pupils can leave a lesson with a clear sense of direction and achievement. Many pupils find that using a computer in their language lessons does provide them with a stimulating and engaging dimension that helps them **make connections** and consequently learn more effectively.

Jim McElwee alerts us to the pitfalls of ICT use and provides practical illustrations on how it can be used to support pupils' learning and teachers' teaching. Why do pupils find ICT motivating? It is so much more than novelty value.

At Dörnyei's teacher-specific motivational component level (teacher-pupil relationship; the teacher's approach to behaviour management; the promotion of sharing ideas and views; provision of motivating feedback):

- ICT allows the teacher to be a 'facilitator';
- it promotes learner autonomy, as pupils make their own choices and identify aspects of language which **they** want to know about;
- it offers the teacher more opportunities for one-to-one support and for providing positive feedback.

'For the first time I feel like I'm getting somewhere.'

At the learner level (development of pupils' self-confidence; information-processing and problem solving strategies):

- the pupils' focus on the screen helps them see patterns and make connections; it facilitates the moving and changing of text; no need for crossing out and erasing;
- it gives pupils the opportunity to enjoy success with writing, an opportunity which may be denied them in pen and paper exercises by the intrusion of the teacher's corrections in red.

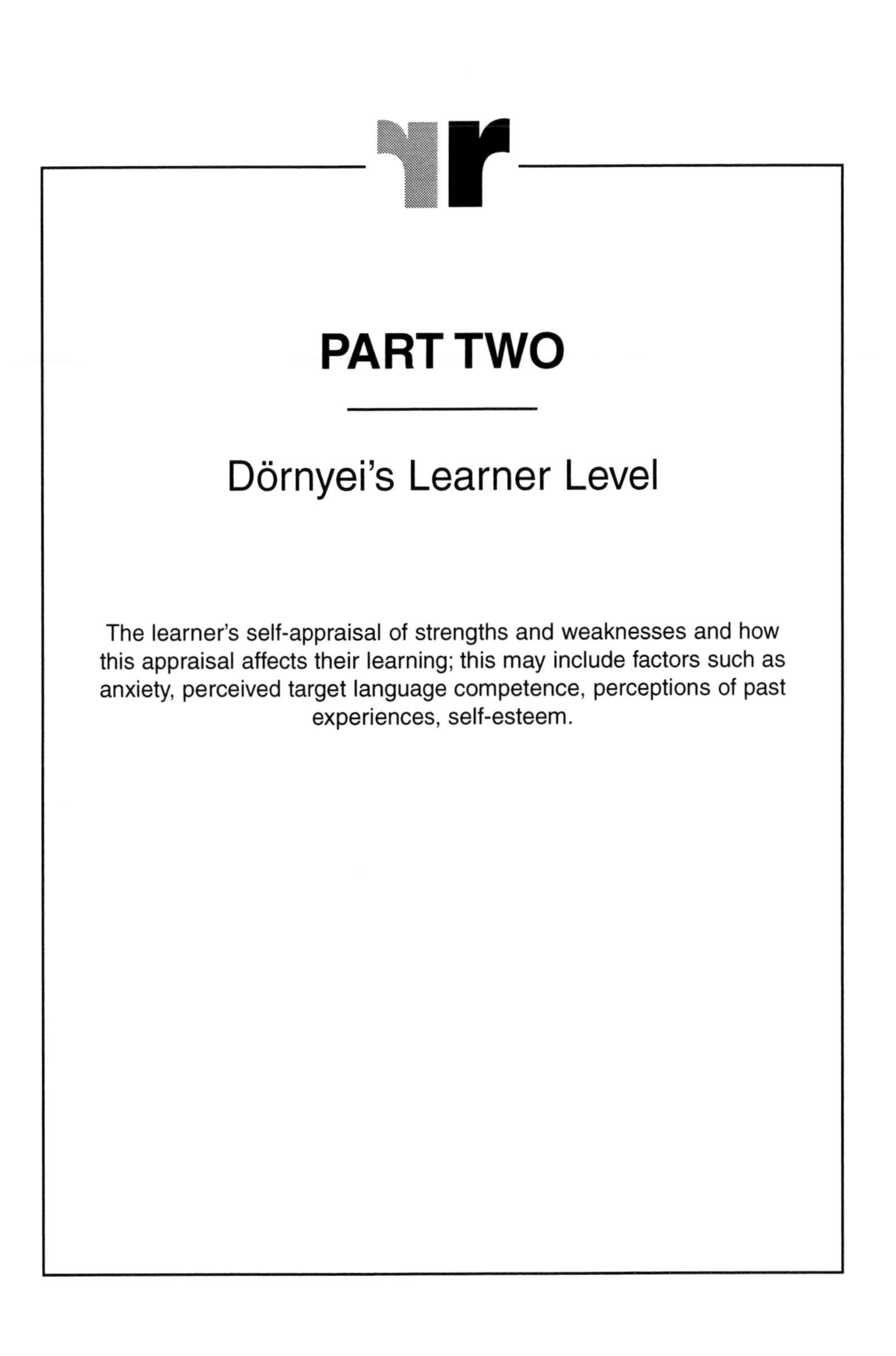

PART TWO

Dörnyei's Learner Level

The learner's self-appraisal of strengths and weaknesses and how this appraisal affects their learning; this may include factors such as anxiety, perceived target language competence, perceptions of past experiences, self-esteem.

Chapter 7

Metacognition and motivation – learning to learn

Terry Lamb

Terry Lamb reflects on how the challenge of disaffection can be tackled by the promotion of learner autonomy. An autonomous learner is, by definition, a motivated learner. This can be translated onto Gardner's socio-educational framework and Dörnyei's framework to provide a motivational template applicable to most classrooms.

Introduction

The aim of this chapter is to examine ways in which learners may be given opportunities to engage with learning, by encouraging them both to see themselves as learners and to be actively involved in the learning process. It examines how this is supported by motivation theory and suggests that we need to think less about ways of motivating learners and more about ways of helping learners to motivate themselves.

Intrinsic and extrinsic motivation

Intrinsic motivation is the desire to learn for its own sake. Of course most children will not be driven towards education if teachers rely on intrinsic motivation alone. Learning is sometimes not enjoyable, as van Lier points out:

> *Will students who are left to rely on interest alone ever progress from Nintendo to Shakespeare?* (van Lier, 1996: 115)

This can lead to demotivation. A typical teacher response when faced with demotivated learners is to tighten up on classroom management and to stimulate extrinsic motivation by means of the introduction of reward systems, such as merits, stickers and certificates and other incentives for learning. Van Lier, however, points to two possible problems with this: firstly, there could be the temptation to reward where inappropriate in an attempt to boost self-esteem, thereby underestimating the learners' ability to evaluate themselves; secondly, there is the possibility that the reward might actually undermine intrinsic motivation, as Sternberg suggests:

> *When you give extrinsic rewards for certain kinds of behavior, you tend to reduce children's interest in performing those behaviors for their own sake. (Sternberg, 1990: 144, quoted in van Lier, 1996: 116).*

Extrinsic rewards need to be handled carefully and always with the long-term goal of developing intrinsic motivation, i.e. moving from motivating learners to helping learners to motivate themselves.

According to Deci and Ryan (1991: 327), intrinsic motivation is inherent in human beings, and based on an innate need for *competence, relatedness,* and *autonomy*. In other words, everyone needs to experience success, to be able to connect with others and have control over their own lives. This would seem to be reinforced by the research of Rudduck *et al* (1996: 47–49) highlighting the need for 'connectedness' i.e. pupils' awareness of where learning activities are heading, why they are being asked to do them, and how they relate to their lives outside school. If we are to tap into our learners' intrinsic motivation, it would seem that there are particular practical implications of these theories:

(i) Work needs to be fully differentiated to cater for all individual needs. Learners need to feel challenged but also competent. In order to manage this in the classroom, learners need to take some responsibility for making choices about their learning (Lamb, 1997).

(ii) Praise needs to be offered, and rewards and incentives are important, but they need to be meaningful and underpinned by learners' own self-assessment.

(iii) Sanctions to tighten up on classroom management must be used judiciously. In a context where learners feel alienated from education and powerless in the face of their futures, increasing control could backfire and contribute to disaffection and truancy.

(iv) The social dimension of learning must not be forgotten; learners can learn from each other through involvement in groupwork.

(v) Natural interest and curiosity need to be stimulated, through careful development of thinking and problem-solving skills.

(vi) Following on from this, learners need to relate to the content of the language they are learning and be able to incorporate their own interests. This is reinforced by my own research in secondary schools where some learners explained that it is the subject-matter they are referring to, not the language itself, when they complain that languages are 'boring' (fifteen-year olds do not want to talk about their pets!).

(vii) Learners need opportunities to manage their own learning. By being allowed to make decisions about what they are doing, their commitment to work can increase (Lamb, 1998).

(viii) Learners need to develop an understanding of the purposes of specific learning tasks, so that they can relate them to their own needs and select appropriately, rather than simply doing them to get merits.

(ix) In order to be able to develop a sense of achievement as well as being able to evaluate themselves and work more autonomously, learners need to develop an understanding of how they learn, and learn how to learn more effectively.

(x) Learners need to be given the opportunity to reflect on the place of learning in their lives in order to encourage connectedness in the broader sense. Focusing on the vocational aspects of language learning without such broader reflection may in fact be counter-productive if learners have a family background of unemployment.

The development of learner autonomy is a key aspect in combating disaffection. Far from increasing control, the teacher needs to empower the learner to be able to work more independently. Teachers need to refocus their efforts away from their own teaching and more onto their learners' learning (Lamb, 1998). They need to rethink their role in motivating learners, with a view to encouraging self-motivation.

So how can teachers encourage their learners to relate more to learning, as well as being more competent and autonomous?

Strategies to develop metacognition

Metacognition can be defined as the learners' knowledge about learning and understanding of and control over the way in which they learn, both in the broader sense of learning styles, and in the more specific areas of learning strategies. It also includes the self-management processes of planning, monitoring and evaluating learning. Research is increasingly providing evidence of the link between metacognition and successful language learning. O'Malley and Chamot (1990: 8), for example, state:

> *Students without metacognitive approaches are essentially learners without direction or opportunity to plan their learning, monitor their progress, or review their accomplishments and future learning directions.*

Without metacognition a learner cannot connect with learning and is unable to be autonomous, and can thus become demotivated. How can learners be encouraged to develop metacognition?

Putting learning styles on the agenda

Learning styles have been defined by Wenden (1991: 36) as including '*cognitive, affective and physiological behaviors that indicate learners' characteristic and consistent way of perceiving, interacting with and responding to the learning environment*'. In other words, they refer to broad characteristics which lead learners to learn in certain individual ways.

Johnston and Dainton (1997), in their *Let Me Learn* programme, prefer to talk about '*learning combinations*' or '*learning patterns*' rather than learning styles, in recognition of the idea that the ways in which we learn are complex, combining different approaches. Some of us like to manage our learning very carefully, some enjoy detail and facts, some prefer to work by doing, some are creative. All of us are a combination of the four, even though we may try to avoid our least preferred approach.

Regardless of the way in which learning styles are defined, however, they offer the possibility of putting learning on the agenda for all of our learners. Johnston and Dainton provide questionnaires or quizzes designed to raise the learners' awareness of the ways in which they learn best. Learners can see that they all have certain strengths. This is one step in the direction of learner empowerment, since they become aware of the kind of environment and activities which are conducive to their learning and, given the opportunity, can negotiate with the teacher for more appropriate learning experiences. It offers a basis for dialogue, raising issues about learning which otherwise may remain unspoken and misunderstood.

By providing such opportunities to talk about learning, disaffected youngsters can be encouraged to perceive themselves as learners. In this way, a connection with learning can be established. Furthermore, the insights which emerge will enable both teacher and student to provide learning experiences which are more appropriate for the individual, thereby increasing the possibility of success and decreasing feelings of alienation from the learning process.

Learner training in learning strategies

Learning strategies are defined by Oxford (1990) in the following way:

> *... learning strategies are operations employed by the learner to aid the acquisition, storage, retrieval, and use of information... learning strategies are specific actions taken by the learner to make learning easier, faster, more enjoyable, more self-directed,*

more effective, and more transferable to new situations. (op.cit.: 8)

As with learning styles, there are many ways of classifying learning strategies. Oxford usefully divides them into 'direct' and 'indirect' strategies. 'Direct' strategies are likened to the performer in a stage play working directly with the language, memorising, understanding and producing it. 'Indirect' strategies are like the director of the play, coordinating the learning process (the performance) by helping learners to focus, organise, check, correct and motivate themselves, acting as an '*internal guide and support to the Performer*' (p.16). In a teacher-centred classroom, the latter are roles largely taken on by the teacher. Teachers, for example, have usually been the ones to correct errors. I would argue that these strategies should be developed in our learners so that they become less dependent on the teacher and more in charge of their own learning. They also offer the possibility of developing skills that can be transferred to other areas of learning, work and life in general.

Take, for example, listening strategies. Intensive listening involves the listener in very careful, detailed listening, for the purpose of understanding much of what is heard; extensive listening involves listening for gist and can involve considerable amounts of inference or even guesswork. Young learners, however, tend not to be aware of this and bring to listening activities an expectation that they should always understand everything. This can lead to loss of confidence, with learners giving up as soon as they lose track.

In order to build confidence and enable learners to listen to new language with a more open mind, it is useful to talk about how to listen. The teacher could play some unknown language (German learners could listen to some Russian, for example), and ask learners firstly to guess (or rather infer) what it is about and then to add any other details. By asking learners to explain how they made sense of the language, they are made more aware of how to listen successfully. It is then possible to offer specific practice in certain strategies. For example, children do not always recognise cognates and near cognates as easily as we do. Words such as *télévision* (in French) or *Italien* (in German) may seem obvious to the teacher, but not to a child who is not used to listening so flexibly. By encouraging them to infer what individual words (such as the months in German) might mean, while pointing out that they will not sound exactly the same as in English, learners are taught strategies which they can apply by themselves.

Such strategy training can be integrated very easily into normal language lessons (for further examples see Oxford, 1990 and Harris, 1997). By asking learners to share the strategies they used in order to learn vocabulary, for example, and encouraging them to try one of their friends' techniques next time, learners will become aware that learning can be done in different ways, enabling them to experiment with alternative, possibly more successful, strategies. On a more sophisticated level, such strategy training can be built into the departmental scheme of work as a long-term, coherent process of development.

Self-management of learning

As a secondary school teacher I sometimes experienced difficulty in getting students to do as I wished. Working through a range of practice activities in the order I specified could result in a great deal of wasted time and some frayed nerves. In a moment of desperation (which was also partly caused by not having enough books to go round the class), I wrote a list of activities on the board, but this time asked the class to do them in any order they liked. The result was a significant increase in the amount of work done.

Deciding to build on this, I started to add to the choice of activity, ensuring that activities also covered speaking and listening, not just reading and writing. One consequence was that students did not all complete the same work at the same time. This situation, combined with a frustration that the time spent marking work did not seem to result in much improvement, led me to produce answer sheets to enable learners to mark at least comprehension activities themselves.

Over a longer period of time, this approach to learning developed into a highly sophisticated, flexible learning scheme, which was adopted by the whole department. From the beginning of Year 7, students had increasing opportunities to make decisions about what they were learning, when they were doing it, and how they approached it. Study guides were developed to enable students to see the objectives of the unit of work (in the form of 'I can ...' statements), and the activities (graded according to difficulty) which related to these objectives. They were also used to record work completed and marks obtained, and to set targets for development. Students were thus involved in self-management of their work, and this included setting up the classroom, getting out resources and equipment and choosing appropriate homework.

This scheme has been described more fully elsewhere (Lamb, 1998). It is a form of 'self-access learning' which is becoming increasingly popular around the world as a way of improving linguistic achievement, independent thinking skills (for example, in Malaysia: see Lamb, 1998a) and motivation. Current research (not yet published) into student attitudes towards this way of learning is revealing positive responses to involvement in decision-making as well as awareness of the advantages of being able to work in a differentiated way. However, it must be stressed that the teacher has to teach the learners the skills of self-management, including better quality decision-making, so that learners know why they are choosing specific tasks. In this way, students are encouraged to talk about their learning needs, negotiate with the teacher and with other students (e.g. for collaborative tasks or tasks which require use of equipment), and are able to work at an appropriate level. Such a way of working responds to both research into disaffection and 'connectedness' (Rudduck *et al*, 1996), and intrinsic motivation and the need for '*competence, relatedness and autonomy*' (Deci *et al*, 1991) as described earlier in this chapter.

Conclusion

Ways need to be found of increasing pupils' sense of responsibility for their learning, of enabling them to relate more to the learning process and to seeing themselves as learners. By encouraging pupils to be aware of some of the issues which surround learning, such as different learning styles and learning strategies, and to be involved in managing the learning environment, teachers hand over some of the control of, and responsibility for, learning. This enables pupils to find the space to enjoy greater success and motivation.

In the context of the National Curriculum in England and Wales, teachers themselves have felt increasingly unable to innovate, and have themselves felt disempowered. The examples above will hopefully show that there are ways in which teachers can respond to the needs of their learners in a creative way while still fulfilling statutory requirements. It is vital that we continue to reflect critically on teaching and learning processes if we are to 'connect' with our learners.

Lamb's practical strategies work because of their sound theoretical underpinning. They relate to Gardner's socio-educational model in the following ways:

Individual differences: these focus on four types of individual differences which influence achievement directly: a) intelligence (speed of learning); b) language aptitude (cognitive and verbal abilities); c) motivation (effort and desire); d) situational anxiety (inhibitions).

Learning outcomes: a) linguistic outcomes – proficiency in the language/grammar/vocabulary/pronunciation/fluency etc; b) non-linguistic outcomes – the attitudes and values which derive from the experience.

The relationship to Dörnyei's framework is even clearer:

at the language level	instrumental motivation
at the learner level	the role of praise and success the promotion of self-efficacy; learning strategies; problem-solving strategies the promotion of favourable self-perception the creation of a non-punitive environment self-evaluation
at the learning situation level	relevance involvement/group work differentiation
teacher-specific motivational components	be a facilitator promote autonomy stimulate intrinsic motivation and internalise extrinsic motivation

group-specific motivation	negotiate with students and agree modes of behaviour encourage each student to be the best that s/he can be; use co-operative learning techniques

There is so much to consider. To neglect one level may well provide the crack which leads to the crumbling of the motivational structure. Most teachers are doing most of these things already, without necessarily being conscious of it. So skilled are they at their job, that they act and react without needing to think about it. This chapter serves to raise awareness which may lead to success in contexts which to date have proven challenging.

Bibliography

Deci E L and R M Ryan, 'A motivational approach to self: integration in personality' in Dienstbier R A (ed), *Perspectives on motivation.* Nebraska Symposium on Motivation, 1990, Vol 38: 237–88 (Lincoln: University of Nebraska Press, 1991)

Deci E L, R J Vallerand, L G Pelletier and R M Ryan, 'Motivation and education: The self-determination perspective' in *Educational Psychologist*, Vol26 (3 and 4): 325–46 (1994)

Johnston C.A. and G.R. Dainton, *Let me learn* (University of New Jersey, 1997)

Harris V, *Pathfinder 31: Teaching learners how to learn: strategy training in the ML classroom* (CILT, 1997)

Lamb T E, 'Self-management strategies in the secondary school languages curriculum' in *Proceedings of the international conference 'AUTONOMY 2000': the development of learning independence in language learning,* held at King Mongkut's Institute of Technology, Thonburi, Bangkok, Thailand, in association with the British Council: 101–15 (November 1996)

Lamb T E, 'Now you are on your own! Developing independent language learning strategies' in Gewehr, W (ed), *Aspects of modern language teaching in Europe*: 30–47 (Routledge, 1998)

Lamb T E, "Learning how to learn' in Malaysia' in *IATEFL Issues,* 144: 14–15 (1998)

Lamb T E, 'Finding a voice – learner autonomy and teacher education in an urban school' in Sinclair, B, I McGrath and T Lamb (eds), *Learner autonomy, teacher autonomy: future directions* (Addison Wesley Longman, forthcoming)

O'Malley J M and A U Chamot, *Learning strategies in second language acquisition* (Cambridge University Press, 1990)

Oxford R L, *Language learning strategies: what every teacher should know* (Boston, Mass: Heinle and Heinle, 1990)

Rudduck J, R Chaplain and G Wallace (eds), *School improvement: what can pupils tell us?* (David Fulton, 1996)

Sternberg R J, 'Prototypes of competence and incompetence', in Sternberg, R J and J Kolligian (eds), *Competence considered*: 117–145 (New Haven: Yale University Press, 1990

Van Lier L, *Interaction in the languages classroom: awareness, autonomy and authenticity* (Longman, 1996)

Chapter 8

A more adult way of learning

Kim Brown

The next two chapters share with Terry Lamb's much of the same philosophy. Kim Brown and Jenifer Alison focus on combatting disaffection by giving more responsibility to the pupils and helping them see the relevance of what they are doing. Again the relationship to Dörnyei's framework, at the Learner level in particular, is very strong.

The context: two classroom research projects

This chapter reviews two classroom research projects which dramatically changed pupils' feelings about learning French. They were developed in direct response to the disaffected behaviour of pupils in a Year 8 and a Year 10 group and both set out to challenge pupils in their negative attitudes to language learning.

The projects were informed by research on active learning strategies[1] and cross-curricular approaches to teaching modern languages.[2] The aim was to engage pupils in topics and issues relating to their local communities that interested and concerned them and to let their language learning needs grow from these projects. The Year 8 pupils were asked to grow sunflower plants at school and to care for them, while the Year 10 pupils were given a wide range of cross-curricular tasks about their local community. There was a broad environmental element to each project, although the purpose went further than simply raising pupils' awareness of green issues. It was much more about encouraging their participation in school, which would, in turn, help them to understand the contribution they could make to shaping the world in which they live. As such, the approach reflects more a commitment to the broad education of young people as active citizens – education for environmental citizenship (Smyth, 1995) – than to environmental awareness in its own right.

We need to understand how we can help more of the pupils in our lessons to feel this sense of involvement in their language learning. It is hoped that some of the reflections of the pupils in this chapter will begin to show us the way. At the same time, we need to help teachers to become involved to the same extent in the process of inquiry about effective language teaching. By including extracts from the journal I kept on the Year 10 project, we gain an appreciation of some of the challenges involved in making changes to our practice and of the kind of support teachers need to do this.

Languages in the curriculum?

In many ways, the case studies in this chapter are not new at all. The projects are informed by research on cross-curricular approaches to language teaching and on independent learning that has been carried out in language classrooms over the last twenty years or so. But there is one aspect of both of these projects which makes them highly relevant to the current context. They were both developed in direct response to the disaffected behaviour of pupils and both sought to challenge these pupils in their perceptions of what was possible in language lessons.

Two government initiatives developed in response to widespread disaffection of young people[3] would appear to have significant implications for languages. Firstly, there is the decision to allow the disapplication of pupils from National Curriculum requirements in Key Stage 4.[4] Where schools have a successful work-related programme in place, pupils who are '*in danger of becoming disaffected or have not experienced much success at school or who have ceased to believe in themselves*' may be allowed to give up two out of three subjects from science, design and technology and modern foreign languages.

Then there are the proposals for the introduction of citizenship into the curriculum.[5] This has not threatened the place of languages and other subjects, as was initially feared,[6] but will inevitably lead to pressures on time in schools to deliver the full curriculum. Subject areas where disaffection is high are likely to be the most vulnerable in any reassessment of teaching time allocations.

The paradox here is that modern foreign languages have the potential to address all of the learning aims set out for these new government initiatives. Far from letting disaffection threaten the place of languages in the curriculum, we need to respond to it by redefining the contribution that our subject area has to make to the education of young people in school.

What does disaffection mean?

For the purposes of this chapter, disaffection is seen in the continued presence of pupils in lessons in which they have no interest at all.

The disaffection in the Year 8 group was characterised by repeated disruption to lessons, dysfunctional relationships between pupils, a refusal to engage in interactions with the teacher and generally negative attitudes to learning French. This was a bottom set, with twice as many boys as girls in the group. The range of learning needs was wide and the level of self-esteem low. The Year 10 group, on the other hand, was a top set. They were co-operative and generally positive in their relationships with each other and with their teacher. The problem was that they displayed absolutely no enthusiasm for the tasks and activities that were set for them. Everything that they did was half-hearted and they would cheerfully admit that French was their least favourite subject. Although both projects were prompted by a determination to challenge these pupils' views of language learning, the level of the challenge in each case was quite different.

If we are going to understand the significance of the changes that took place, we need to have a clear picture of what was going on in the classroom before the project started.

Whole class teaching

The biggest change to the way of working for these pupils was the move from whole class teaching to small group and pair work.

For the Year 10 pupils, whole class teaching was quite simply boring:

> *If a teacher just tells us the information and we copy off the board or sheets, this is much more boring; and if something is boring, it is harder to learn because I'm not interested, so this was a good change.*

But there was another dimension to their dislike of this way of working: some of the pupils found whole class teaching threatening. The following comments are typical:

> *... when the teacher is talking I get lost easily and don't understand and so I think I am thick and give up trying and I start looking around, getting bored and so I don't learn anything and I'm too shy to ask for help in front of a whole class but when we work in small groups or as individuals I don't mind asking for help so I learn more.*

Year 10 pupils were clearly not comfortable in whole class teaching situations and they talked of the change in teaching style in terms of *less pressure*:

> *Recent French lessons have been different as we have been going at our own speed. We have not been pressured, and our projects have been entirely our own doing.*

Year 8 pupils reacted much more strongly against whole-class teaching. The behaviour of individuals was so unpredictable that even with two teachers in the room it was often difficult to maintain a purposeful working atmosphere. The worse the behaviour, the less we felt able to offer the class anything but the most controlled classroom activities. In the event, it was clear that this insistence on whole class teaching was part of the problem. There were two other challenges:

- the pupils' resistance to the target language;
- the feeling of being somehow *cooped up* in the classroom.

How these challenges were met is revealed in the description of the projects below.

The projects and their implications

In this section, we shall focus on three main characteristics of the projects which seemed to contribute to the heightened levels of motivation in the pupils:

- the element of trust and the changing role of the teacher implicit in this new way of working;
- the cross-curricular aspects of the projects;
- the individual triumphs of the pupils in these lessons.

The element of trust

Clearly, there was a large element of risk in this kind of project. The Year 8 pupils were to be given seeds to plant, and asked to measure and record their rate of growth. They gave no reassurance that they could be trusted to behave sensibly in the classroom let alone outside with spades and watering cans and bags of compost. Nor was there any evidence that they would respond positively to a project on their environment. They had little regard for the state of their classroom and would risk being kept behind after school rather than pick up pieces of paper in their room that they had not dropped. If the project was going to work, there had to be a strong element of trust in it.

A decision had to be made: did we lay down elaborate rules and sanctions in case of misbehaviour before the project began or did we wait to see what happened? We chose the latter. The wisdom of this decision was confirmed by the entirely changed behaviour of the pupils from the first day. They took the project very seriously: they were well behaved in the school grounds, they took care of my camera, they returned to the classroom at specified times and sat down to work on their weather charts and bar graphs without being told. In short, the absence of rules implied that we expected and believed that they could behave sensibly and they responded to this trust. This goes back to the discussion on whole class teaching: is it the case that the more we insist on control of the pupils, the less chance they have to show us that they can behave independently and responsibly?

They had no reason to pull against the activities we set them as they could interpret them in their own way. They were asked to record the weather in French each week; to present this information in graph or bar chart form; to take photographs of their plants as they grew and to write labels and captions, speech bubbles and questions around their photographs, all in French; they wrote French poems about their environment and about the process of growing things. The aim was to give them more opportunities to practise basic language and number skills through repeated work on the same topic.

We shall see in the next section how they valued, in particular, the practical element of the tasks. The use of photographs as visual stimuli for their language work introduced a new and motivating dimension to their lessons[7]: instead of pupils ignoring my arrival in the classroom as had previously been the case, they were now crowding round my desk to see the photographs of their plants. Such a change in attitude must make us think again about the ways in which we are teaching languages to whole classes of pupils. Above all, it is the opportunity to cater for individual learning needs through a range of tasks and activities that emerges as the key factor of the success of these projects.

This is particularly evident in the comments and reflections of the pupils in the Year 10 group. They had been asked to complete a range of tasks on their local environment: for example, to conduct a survey in French, to interview individuals about their attitudes to their local environment, or take a photograph of some aspect of their local community that interested them and write a commentary on it in French. They worked in pairs or small groups and had three weeks to complete the tasks. Many of the pupils found this a motivating way of working:

> *You had to use your own initiative, work things out for yourself.*
>
> *Taking responsibility for my work, working for myself. Not obliged to do it for the teacher's sake I feel gives a better attitude to learning. You learn at your own pace and you get out what you put in ... my theory is that if people feel they want to learn they will.*

As well as encouraging positive attitudes to work in general, there was a recognition that this independence helped individual pupils specifically with their language learning:

> *This way of learning French is better as we were given a lot of responsibility for our own learning. In this way of learning it made us think more carefully whether things made sense and to correct our own mistakes.*

However, there were two pupils in the group (out of 28) who did not enjoy this way of working:

> *I have only learned to say words like things to do with buildings ... I find it easier to learn from a teacher.*

> *I have not found this very easy compared to the normal learning techniques and would prefer them.*

Because the majority of the class were working well, I was able to take these pupils aside and provide them with a structured programme of tasks each week. In other words, the flexibility of the classroom organisation freed me up and gave me the opportunity to cater more sensitively to the wide range of needs across the group.

THE CHANGING ROLE OF THE TEACHER

Reading again my journal from the early days of the Year 10 project, I was struck by the extent to which I was the one who seemed to be finding this new approach difficult. There were frequent references to the frustration I felt when pupils did not seem to be working fast or hard enough, or when they did not make as much use of the support materials I had devised for them as I felt they ought to be doing. A few extracts from my notes from the early days of the project give a flavour of my reflections at that time:

> *Frustrations – for the first twenty minutes or so, no-one came to ask for documentation to support the activities, they seemed not to understand the notion of a resource bank or of getting out of their seats and asking for support materials.*

> *Another frustration here is that two of the most able girls chose to start with the poster activity – which I feel is less useful for them than a more challenging activity, e.g. recording an interview. It would be interesting to know why pupils start where they do. Does it matter? What is the purpose of the project?*

It is clear that I was finding it difficult to relinquish the role I was used to and to see value in the things that the pupils valued and wanted to do. By lesson two, I had begun to acknowledge that some of my frustrations were simply a reflection of my reluctance to let go of these pupils:

> *Arrived to find the class already working in groups on their chosen tasks. Brilliant! Spoilt it by interrupting and getting them to do a survey on leisure activities that had been planned ... perhaps I am finding it hard to let go completely.*

In the same way, I can still remember the sense of disorientation I felt when the Year 8 group began to measure each other with metre rules and record their findings: they were all on task and had forgotten I was there. The point here is that while these projects were designed to challenge the pupils' perceptions of language learning, they were also beginning to challenge my perceptions of my role as a language teacher. Moreover, these were the feelings of a teacher who was fully convinced of the rationale for this approach and who really wanted these projects to be successful. It is perhaps not surprising that teachers who are not convinced to the same extent of a need to change their practice find it difficult to do so.

A cross-curricular approach to language learning

The pupils were clearly trying to make sense of the new experiences they were being offered in language lessons. This is reflected in the ways in which they express themselves in their evaluations. It was not like *normal lessons* (Hustler, Milroy and Cockett 1991) and yet they were still doing all these things in French.

> *The sunflower project was fun because we got out of some of the French lessons but my plant is not that big.*

> *Some of the work we did was a bit different like estimating a metre. People in other classes said it was nothing to do with French but you learned a lot.*

A number of the pupils borrowed terminology from their science lessons – practicals – to describe their experiences. They knew that growing sunflowers in French was in some way different, that it was *blurring the boundaries* (Black *et al*, 1996) between different curriculum subjects and this is reflected in their use of language:

> *When we started our project on sunflowers and first planted them I thought it could be quite good to do instead of doing lots of writing. I feel that I have learned a lot about this because it was done as a practical instead of pages and pages of writing. I found this way a lot easier to learn the French.*

By bringing into language lessons topics and tasks which pupils more readily associate with other curriculum areas, we can begin to challenge their assumptions about what constitutes a typical language lesson. We might, for example, try to build in opportunities for pupils to represent their findings of a class survey in bar graph form or on the computer so that they experience the same degrees of success in language lessons as in other curriculum areas. Furthermore, if a broader approach to language learning tasks means that pupils can show their language teachers the things they do well in other subject areas, this might also begin to challenge language teachers' perceptions of their pupils' abilities. In other words, where a pupil might appear to be unsuccessful and disaffected in language lessons, this kind of evidence can help teachers to question the nature of the tasks that they are setting pupils rather than the attitude of the pupils themselves to the tasks.

In addition, a cross-curricular approach can offer pupils an opportunity to consolidate in language lessons their learning in other areas of the curriculum. A Year 8 pupil, for example, discovered that she did not know how many centimetres were in a metre. As her plant grew towards a hundred centimetres, she began to realise her uncertainty about the way the numbers worked. The project gave her a further opportunity to clarify her understanding of concepts she had met, but not wholly understood, in her maths lessons, in the context of a real task and in French.

The pupils in both year groups were keenly aware of the ways in which this cross-curricular approach had changed their experiences of learning. Year 10 pupils were able to identify many areas of personal achievement during the project:

> *Learned to do things by myself without you telling me what to do.*
>
> *I have learned more about my environment at school. Also I have learned how to draw up a timetable on the computer.*
>
> *I did also learn to get on with some more different people while doing the project.*
>
> *Firstly, I have learned to use a video camera properly ...*

Individual triumphs of the pupils

The phrase comes from my journal of the Year 10 project:

> *What I am noticing is that in each lesson so far there has been a small personal triumph for different individual pupils.*

A typical entry from my diary gives an idea of the kind of achievement that these *triumphs* might represent:

> *The resource centre is beginning to work much better now. I have produced a support sheet with key questions to ask in French and pupils are using this and are getting confidence to come up. One pupil came up first, couldn't ask for what he wanted, went away with the sheet, came back and asked correctly for something – that in fact, I did not have – went away again and came back on two more occasions to ask for different things, each time asking the question Est-ce que vous pouvez me donner ... correctly and with growing confidence (not using the sheet to read from). I can safely say that he has learned this and is confident using it now. This is a boy who rarely says anything in class.*

On another occasion I noted down the things I learned about individual pupils' personal circumstances. Here is an example:

> *I learned more today about individual pupils in twenty minutes than in eight weeks of teaching: namely, that one girl's mum is French-speaking and has lived most of her life in Switzerland and Egypt – she can interview her mum on the environment. Interesting that I have had no notion that this pupil has such close contact with a French speaker.*

Similarly, when the project ended and pupils handed in their work, I was struck by the range of tasks they had completed:

> *It was much more exciting to collect in video and audio tapes, posters and leaflets, pie charts and statistics and photographs than a uniform pile of exercise books. All this work felt much more personal and valued.*

The pupils, too, were aware of the richness of their individual learning experiences, particularly in terms of their enhanced understanding of language.

> *I have improved my knowledge of 'joining' words and I think that I have generally improved my French.*

> *I've learned a lot about my weaknesses in writing, forgetting plurals, etc and how to phrase things. I did a lot of writing about the same types of things, so I've noticed mistakes that I consistently made and hopefully have learned them correctly now.*

The effectiveness of the sunflower project is in part reflected in the photographs that the pupils themselves took as the project unfolded. Here we see groups of pupils gently planting their seedlings in the open ground; we see photographs of a pair of trainers alongside a seedling as pupils found novel ways of showing the relative size of their plants; we see boys proudly showing off their healthy plants to the camera. The photographs are valuable evidence of the ways in which this project changed the way that these pupils felt about language lessons and about themselves.

Conclusion: a growing problem

The sense of achievement that pupils experienced through taking care of their own plants helped them to feel more positive about themselves. This, in turn, helped them to relate more successfully to each other.

The poor behaviour and the idle, sexual taunts all disappeared as the pupils went into action, watering, measuring and recording the growth of their plants. Not once did any of the pupils (and most of them were boys) complain about growing flowers; boys' renewed sense of positive self-esteem made it *OK* to grow flowers and to work with girls in a constructive and supportive way.

Above all, the emphasis in these projects was on helping these pupils to experience a sense of caring, and to build on this in helping them to engage in lessons. The focus in language lessons tends to be on cognitive skills, on knowing about language and how to use it: it may be that we need to recognise the opportunities to address the affective dimensions of young people's learning if we are to fully engage them in our lessons.[8] In the words of one Year 10 pupil:

> *Yes, I much prefer this. It brings French to life. Dealing with real life topics which actually mean something...it's a more adult way of learning and means you can possibly enjoy it.*

A broader approach to language teaching would need the following:

- a focus on broad educational aims in language lessons to enhance the development of pupils' understanding, skills, values and beliefs as well as their knowledge;
- a range of teaching and learning styles in our lessons to cater for individual needs;
- opportunities to link with other subject areas in the planning, delivery and assessment of our lessons.

In this way, we can make a strong argument for the place of languages in the whole curriculum and for the role it has to play in the preparation of young people for adult life.

Bibliography

Black P & J M Atkin, Eds. *Changing the Subject, Innovations in Science, Mathematics and Technology Education,* (Routledge,1996)

Bentley T *Learning beyond the classroom* London (Routledge, 1998)

Brown K Citizens of a disappearing world (*TES, June*1998)

Brown K & M Brown, *New contexts for Modern Language Learning: cross-curricular approaches,* (CILT,1996)

Brown, K. & M Brown, *Changing Places, Cross-curricular approaches to teaching languages,* Resource file 1, (CILT,1998)

DES *Modern Foreign Languages for ages 11–16 Proposals* (DES, 1990)

Gardner H, *Frames of mind* (Fontana, 1983)

Gardner H, *Multiple intelligences – the theory in practice* (New York: Basic Books, 1993)

Goleman D, *Emotional intelligence: Why it can matter more than IQ* (Bloomsbury, 1996) Hustler D, E Milroy, M Cockett, *Learning Environments for the whole curriculum, 'It's not like normal lessons'* (Unwin Hyman, 1991)

Smyth J, Environment and Education: a view of a changing scene, *Environmental Education Research, 1, No. 1*(1995)

Notes

1 See, for example, Pike G and D Selby, *Global teacher, global learner* (Hodder and Stoughton, 1987).

2 See Brown K and M Brown (1996; 1998) for examples of resources that can be used to support cross-curricular approaches in modern language lessons.

3 See Bentley, T *Learning beyond the classroom,* Routledge 1998, for a useful overview of disaffection in young people in this decade and of the government's responses to it.

4 DfEE The Education (National Curriculum) (Exceptions at Key Stage 4) Regulations 1998 (Statutory Instruments 1998 No 2021) London: DfEE.

5 Following recommendations in the final report of the Advisory group on Citizenship, *Education for citizenship and the teaching of democracy in schools* (QCA 1998) the Secretary of State for Education announced in May 1999 proposals that citizenship lessons for secondary pupils should be compulsory from 2002.

6 See Brown K, *Citizens of a disappearing world, TES, 1998.*

7 For further discussion of the potential of photographs to enhance language learning, see Brown K, 'Developing a new modern languages pedagogy' in Green S (ed) *New perspectives on teaching and learning modern languages,* Multilingual Matters, 2000

8 Recent research on multiple intelligences (Gardner) and emotional intelligence (Goleman) makes a strong case for a broader range of learning aims in formal education.

Chapter 9

A vocational framework and its potential to motivate

Jenifer Alison

Jenifer Alison's chapter again relates closely to Dörnyei's *learner level*. The *language level* also comes across strongly:

> Develop learners' instrumental motivation – discuss the role of the target language in the world, its usefulness to the pupils and to the country. (Dörnyei, 1994: 281)

The links with the other levels of the framework cannot, however, be ignored. Jenifer provides two case studies based on experience with Year 10 pupils.

It is natural for us, as teachers, to strive to do the best for our students. In this climate of ever increasing pressure to 'get results' it can be so puzzling and exasperating when the students are unwilling to go along with us. We can experience disaffection at all levels of ability. At best, it manifests itself in symptoms such as lethargy, unresponsiveness and lack of urgency. At worst, lack of motivation results in disruptive and anti-social behaviour.

It is difficult, often, to get to the bottom of the problem when, for example, a student bursts into the room with, '*Rubbish this – it's boring – can't do it, can I?*' It is perhaps even more difficult to identify the reasons for the behaviour of the withdrawn, dreamy 'could-do-better' member of the class.

How can we instil into all of our learners the desire to learn and progress? Effective teaching cannot be dismissed as merely a product of individual charisma (Cooper *et al*, 1994: 130). Rather than focus on our persona, would it not be better to focus on the learning experience of our students and develop our professional skills to help turn things round?

What can we learn from the literature about motivation?

In the 1970s Gardner and Lambert (1972) suggested that motivation for language learning could be divided into two categories:

- integrative orientation: the learner's perceptions of him or herself becoming part of the second language community; for example, making a wider circle of friends in the target language country, travelling there, even living there, adopting the culture and being regarded as 'one of the locals';
- instrumental orientation: learning the language more as a means to an end, for example to achieve higher status within one's own culture, to pass examinations, or to get a better job.

Research based on these orientations sought to discover which was the more powerful. Gardner and Lambert found that motivation with an integrative orientation was more powerfully associated with success. Other researchers, however, for example Burstall (1974), found that instrumental orientation was the stronger force. Which do we think is the more powerful for our less-than-enthusiastic students?

How integratively motivated are our students? Can we reach the stage where they learn the language in order to be part of the target language country and its culture? Perhaps not ('*Don't want to go there anyway!*'). Is the generating of instrumental motivation likely to be any more successful? ('*If you work hard, you'll get a good GCSE grade in two years' time!*'). Many of us will agree that that also has little effect. The students we are thinking about often feel such a lack confidence in their ability that they cannot envisage such distant goals. So, where is the answer? What if we concentrated on an integrative orientation to success, interpreting the term 'integrative' as the students' desire to integrate with a world which is important to them?

This means, rather than focusing on **our** perspective, i.e. feeling enthusiasm for the target language and the people, we would take **their** perspective as a starting point. We could ask them what is important to **them** and how they perceive themselves. Talking to our 14–16-year olds, we often discover that they tend to see themselves as young adults (even though some of them sometimes may have a strange way of showing it). Many will have attended interviews about their future career; many of their pursuits outside school will involve the adult world; many of them will have part-time employment. So, what if we were to use the foreign language as a vehicle for **integration** with the adult working world?

A vocational context?

This introductory statement from a Qualifications and Curriculum Authority (1999) publication gives us food for thought:

> *Learning activities and materials developed through links with local businesses and the wider community can encourage pupils to engage actively with the world of work and help them make connections between what they learn in the classroom and the world outside. Work-related contexts created by teachers working in partnership with businesses and the wider community can powerfully enhance teaching and learning.*

Would a vocational context and approach be the answer to motivation? What might be the possible advantages of establishing a vocational framework to the learning programme?

There are several ways of creating a vocational dimension (see QCA, 1999 for case studies). Alison (1993: 11) and Alison and Bettsworth (1998: 6; 38–42) give further practical guidelines and examples of how vocational projects could be organised. Projects involving links with people and places of work outside school are fundamental to the motivational aspect of the *Certificate of Achievement in Modern Foreign Languages: Skills for Work* (Alison, 1999). The aim of this course is to help students develop linguistic, social, personal and other work-related skills necessary when catering for foreign visitors to Britain. Materials which the students create for the workplace can be assessed as coursework. Below is an example from an optional module, *Working in a Bar or Restaurant*, which gives suggestions for a group project.

A group of 4–5 students could take a particular area of a topic and each contribute a section.

For example:

A brochure for the hotel or conference centre or even the local Macdonald's

This could be a pack showing:

- *opening hours*
- *facilities offered with times and days*
- *leisure activities which are possible, e.g. darts, dominoes*
- *descriptions of drinks*
- *descriptions of dishes on the menu*
- *a price list for drinks in the foreign language*
- *a detailed menu, with descriptions of dishes and prices*
- *a list of useful phrases for foreign clients*
- *a list of useful phrases for the waiter, waitress, or people who work behind the bar.*

The choice is limitless. The very best way to set up the coursework is to take the class to interview people at work in a local bar, restaurant, hotel or conference centre. These are the best people to say what material they need in the foreign language.

Case studies

What follows are two case study extracts illustrating different approaches to implementing the vocational dimension. In extract 1 a teacher gives GCSE work a twist to create a vocational context. In extract 2, a teacher runs the course for the *Certificate of Achievement in Modern Foreign Languages: Skills for Work* alongside GCSE.

CASE STUDY EXTRACT 1

This features a group of 15- to 16-year olds with a very wide range of ability. The teacher examined the existing materials and course book, to find opportunities to create vocational contexts and roles. For instance, she took a reading or listening passage about leisure and sports available in a town, and put the students in the role of tourist office employees who had to interpret the information for a foreign visitor. They made leaflets and posters to show which activities and events were available in their own town. This material was then used in a simulation or role play, in which the tourists asked about what was available in the town and they were provided with information on things to see and do. The students appreciated this vocational twist to their GCSE work. (T: teacher. S1–5: five students' responses)

> **T:** *When we do some of the tasks, I put it into a work-type context. Does that help? Or does it not really make any difference?*
>
> **S.1:** *It helps, because you can imagine yourself in that position.*
>
> **S.2:** *It's sort of like realistic to you.*
>
> **S.3:** *It helps you come up with ideas, if you think that that's the person you are and that's what you are doing now.*
>
> **T:** *So, you like it to be in some sort of work-type context?*
>
> **S.4:** *You think Tourist Office and then you remember the kind of conversation you had in the tourist office – it's just a way of remembering.*
>
> **T:** *If we do a listening task and I say that this is the sort of information you would have to listen for if you found yourself working in a firm or wherever – does that make any difference?*
>
> **S.5:** *Yes, because you want to do it more if you can see why you need it – because if you think that's pretty useless then you don't want to do it.*

The strong message from the students, is that the vocational context means something to them. This motivates them and so they find the language easier to remember.

The teacher in Case Study extract 2 goes a step further by taking the students out of the classroom situation into places of work.

CASE STUDY EXTRACT 2

These 15- to 16-year old students visited local places of work to ask the employees or proprietors which linguistic, personal, social and work-related skills are needed when catering for foreign visitors to Britain. The information gathered formed the basis of the content and context of their lessons. The students carried out projects designed to help the employees in the workplace. Their teacher relates:

> *I divided the class of twenty into groups of three or four. I set up three places to visit. Each member of the group was to go to a different place (e.g. one to a hotel, another to the tourist board, etc). This made three groups of six or seven, which was practical, as some organisations don't want twenty students all at once.*
>
> *Each representative of the original team of three was responsible for collecting information for his or her team mates' projects as well as for his or her own.*

The students, fired with enthusiasm by the projects they had completed for the workplaces, asked their teacher for more visits in their written evaluations:

> *Having outings makes the course more exciting ... Maybe we could undertake more work for companies?*
>
> *I think the course would be improved by having more links with industry/business.*

The visits were highly motivating. There was an additional bonus. Taking part in these visits meant that these girls, many of whom led very sheltered lives, were able to venture out into the working environment in the company of their teacher and friends. This made the later experience of entering the work placement alone far less daunting. Indeed two girls set up their own work experience visits with the hotel they had visited.

A vocational framework seems to work. But what about the classroom reality?

Providing an integrative orientation to achievement (my interpretation rather than Gardner and Lambert's) by setting up a vocational framework for language learning looks promising. Enthusiasm for the foreign language, its people, country(ies) and culture(s) might even grow from this. How does the exploitation of a vocational framework on a day-to-day basis in the classroom help to motivate?

Stevick (1971: 102–7) stresses the importance of **relevance, authenticity** and **satisfaction** (*inter alia)* as criteria for the selection of language teaching materials. These are also important considerations within the vocational framework. Establishing a vocational way of working allows students to demonstrate and develop skills which they see as **relevant** to the working world, that is working independently, setting themselves targets, taking responsibility for their progress, engaging in team work, collaborating on tasks. Carrying out **authentic**, or near authentic tasks, gives meaning to their learning and forges a link with the adult, working world. How then can these considerations be incorporated into our approaches to teaching to give our students a greater sense of **satisfaction**?

Working independently and setting targets

When the class works independently, it leaves us free to circulate and to build up good personal relationships with individual students (Cooper *et al,* 1994: 120). In so doing, we are more likely to discover their different learning needs. Sutton (1991) stresses that:

> *Learners learn at different rates, to different levels of attainment and in different ways. They deserve to be offered equal opportunities to learn and develop, therefore need equal access to the learning experiences we offer and we need to recognise their particular strengths and difficulties.*

Although we are unlikely to be experts in every kind of learning difficulty, getting to know our students better will give us more chance of understanding the background to an individual's reluctance to work and to support him or her in setting realistic targets for progression. This may be facilitated by allowing students regularly to choose tasks at their own level. The pattern in Table 1 below shows how we could organise an aspect of language learning, by using whole-class activities for presentation and assimilation of core language (stages 1 and 2) and then letting students choose from a bank of differentiated tasks (stage 3). Being able to work at their own pace on tasks relevant to their needs, they may be more likely to enjoy the satisfaction of completing work successfully.

Table 1. In this class there are students whose ability ranges from Levels 1–5+.

CONSOLIDATION (Certificate of Achievement)	ALL STUDENTS	EXTENSION (GNVQ/GCSE)
Stage 1	PRESENTATION OF TOPIC AND LANGUAGE	
Stage 2	RECOGNITION, REPETITION, REMEMBERING National Curriculum Levels 2–3	
Stage 3 REINFORCEMENT e.g. more activities: matching cards? ADAPTATION extra materials to support students with learning difficulties	PRACTICE ACTIVITIES e.g. teach and test partner with cue cards ←→	EXTENSION TASKS e.g. Gap information writing sketches
Stage 4 National Curriculum Levels 1–3	USING THE LANGUAGE e.g. for projects, assignments for the place of work ←→	National Curriculum Level 4, 5+

Stage 4 above is taken up again in Table 2. The class collaborate on a project for the local tourist office. Students are made aware of the National Curriculum Level they are targeting when working on their contribution. The important aspect of working this way is that all students have the opportunity to feel that they are making a real contribution to the project, regardless of the level.

Table 2. Open-ended activities for using the language. Topic: *Que peut-on faire ici?*

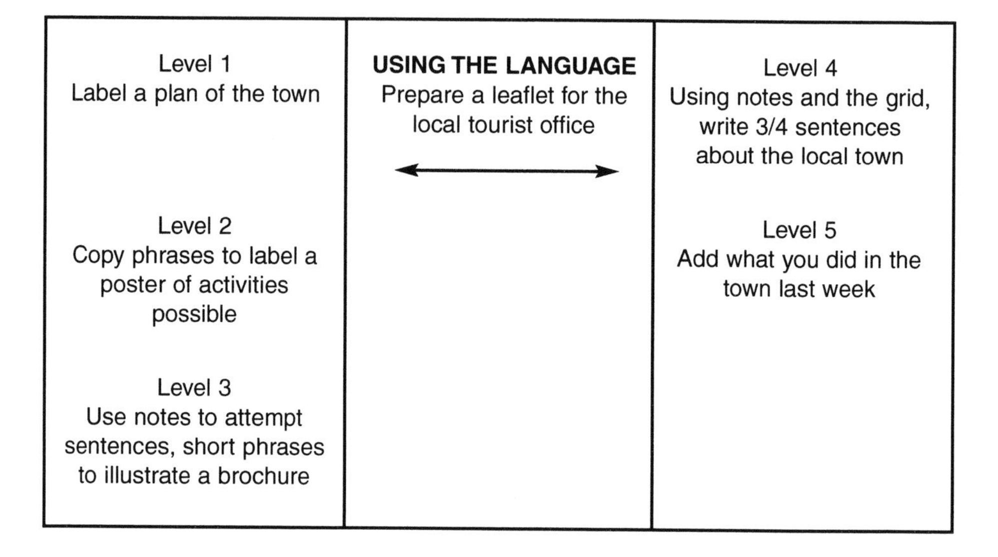

Level 1 Label a plan of the town	**USING THE LANGUAGE** Prepare a leaflet for the local tourist office ⟷	Level 4 Using notes and the grid, write 3/4 sentences about the local town
Level 2 Copy phrases to label a poster of activities possible		Level 5 Add what you did in the town last week
Level 3 Use notes to attempt sentences, short phrases to illustrate a brochure		

Engaging in team work

Working collaboratively can lead to a more relaxed and secure atmosphere in the classroom, where students are willing to help one another, using each other's strengths. A good illustration of this comes from a teacher who set her students off to work in pairs on a listening task. As the students were organising how they were going to do this, she overheard one girl saying to her partner:

> *You listen and I'll write the answers in, because you are better at listening and I'm good at writing.*

Here they were exercising interpersonal skills to negotiate tasks and achieve as a team. Collaborative working allows students to enjoy each other's support. The threat of embarrassment or failure is removed.

Contributing first-hand skills

The more we mirror real-life situations in tasks, the more chance we give students to demonstrate a whole range of skills they may already have. This can boost their self-esteem and persuade them they have an important role to play. Alison (1993: 6–8) gives an example of students who formed a committee to organise the preparation of a brochure in French for the local tourist office. It transpired that one of the members of the group, with a history of disruptive, unco-operative behaviour, was part of the Children in Care Council for his children's home and knew all about committees. He appointed himself chairman of the tourist office project and masterminded the whole production which included, among other of the more predictable items, directions around the town for a 'pub crawl'. He thoroughly enjoyed this key role, and there was a very positive working atmosphere in the room while he was in charge.

Developing communicative skills

In Table 1 above, the practice tasks (Stage 3) are interactional – teach and test partner, information gap, role plays, simulations. Interactional tasks are essential for the development of communicative skills. Students who find listening to the language or speaking it difficult often gain confidence when they are enabled to see that communication does not have to break down when they do not understand, or when words fail them. Much has been written about teaching '*techniques of coping with difficulties in communicating in an imperfectly known second language*' (Stern 1983: 411). For example, the listener can control the speaker by asking for repetition, etc, and the speaker can paraphrase or mime if a word cannot be recalled. These students, who experienced learning difficulties, explain it from their perspective:

> *If you can't say it, you point to a picture of it or draw it. I didn't know the word for 'car', so I drew a picture of one.*
>
> *You can do sign language.*
>
> *If you don't understand what they say, you can say, 'Je ne comprends pas' or you can hold things up to see if that's what they mean. Get them to point to it.*

Could it be that the teacher's emphasis has been so much on 'getting it right' since Year 7 that students do not feel this kind of communication will be acceptable in the classroom?

Personal and social skills

Simulations, role plays and surveys are just a few examples of tasks which will allow students to demonstrate the personal and social skills necessary when catering for foreign visitors. These can be built into the assessment criteria for successful completion. In this way, even if a student does not score very highly for linguistic performance, he or she may achieve recognition for skills such as resourcefulness, charm, or making the foreign visitor feel welcome.

The role of success in motivation

A vocational dimension has the potential to enhance students' motivation. What other, far more down-to earth reason do students have for making a real effort?

One of the most powerful incentives is success: their recognition of their own success; their awareness that their successes are acknowledged. What does this mean in the context of the teaching reality?

Record keeping, apart from being essential, can be an important way in which the teacher and student celebrate success. The differentiated tasks we set should ensure positive marking. Rewards (as appropriate to the maturity of the group) provide a good incentive to work and reflect appreciation of achievement. Some teachers run an accumulative points system, where the individual's points for good work contribute to a class total. For example, when a class totals 200 points a privilege is granted, which could be as simple as permission to play CDs of their choice (quietly) during the next lesson. Success in achieving short-term goals may be recorded on merit certificates or in *Commendation Letters*. These could be stored in the student's *National Record of Achievement* and contribute towards his or her curriculum vitae. Experiencing success motivates the student to progress further and, feeling motivated, he or she is more likely to be successful.

Conclusion

So how true is the QCA's assertion (see above) that allowing students to make connections between what they learn in the classroom and the world outside can powerfully enhance teaching and learning? What has been illustrated here is that when students work in adult contexts in which they can perceive themselves in the future, they find it easier to identify with what they are learning. In setting up vocational ways of working we are allowing them to develop a wide range of competencies in addition to linguistic skills. In allowing them to work independently on manageable tasks, and in recognising their achievements and sharing their sense of pride with them, we give them a chance to experience success. Links with local places of work allow students to interact with adults other than their teachers. These adults have great significance for them because, unaware of the labels some of these students may carry around school, ('*Lazy! Careless! Won't work! Won't learn!*'), they take them at face value. Being in a position to help these people, who often have little or no knowledge of the foreign language, gives students a sense of importance and they are eager to impress. They have the chance now to be labelled with a positive identity. These people have become the 'significant others' (Cooper *et al*, 1994: 142) they needed to help them rebuild their sense of value and self-esteem. Adopting a vocational framework – and exploiting links with local places of work – means we can offer students a new start. Add to this the engaging of our professional skill and understanding in the classroom, and we do have the capacity to turn things round.

So why were Kim Brown's and Jenifer Alison's projects successful?

At the learner level:

they developed pupils' self-confidence;
they created a supportive, accepting, non-punitive learning environment.

At the language level:

they developed learners' instrumental motivation – by illustrating the role of the target language in this country;

At the learning situation level:

they increased pupils' interest and involvement in the tasks;
they facilitated student satisfaction.

Re: teacher-specific motivational components:

they promoted learner autonomy;

Re: group specific motivational components:

they increased the group's goal-orientedness;
they promoted the development of group cohesion
they used co-operative learning techniques.

Circumstances may not allow us to replicate the projects described by Kim and Jenifer. Nonetheless, the principles underpinning their success with their classes apply equally to our less ambitious classroom activities.

Acknowledgements

This chapter has been written after discussions with many teachers and students in schools. Their contribution was invaluable and is greatly appreciated. This includes the teachers who provided the two case studies:

Anna Bartrum, Head of Modern Languages and her Year 10 at St Paul's RC High School, Milton Keynes. (Anna Bartrum is now PGCE Course Leader, St Martin's College, Lancaster.)

Heidi Elliot and her Year 10 at Hodge Hill Girls' School, Birmingham.

Thanks too to Daphne Watt and her Year 10 at Castlederg High School, Castlederg, for providing examples from their evaluation of the *CoA Modern Language Skills for Work* course.

Thanks to Heysham High School in Morecambe and Morton School, Carlisle for allowing the author to work with their Year 9 and Year 10 classes over recent years.

Bibliography

Alison J, *Not Bothered* (CILT, 1993)

Alison J, and Bettsworth B, Handbook 1: *Motivating Students at the Early Stages of Language Learning* (CILT, 1998)

Alison J, *Certificate of Achievement in Modern Foreign Languages: Skills for Work: Module B: Working in a Bar or Restaurant, Part D.* (Languages Development Centre, St Martin's College, 1999)

Burstall C, M Jamieson, S Cohen, M Hargreaves, *Primary French in the Balance* (NFER, 1974)

Cooper P, Smith C J and Upton G, *Emotional and Behavioural Difficulties: Theory to Practice.* (Routledge, 1994)

Hargreaves D, *The Challenge for the Comprehensive School*, (Routledge and Kegan Paul, 1982)

McPake J, R Johnstone, L Low and L Lyall, *Interchange 59: Foreign Languages in the Upper Secondary School: A Study of the Causes of Decline*, (Scottish Office Education and Industry Department, 1999)

Qualification and Curriculum Authority, *Learning through Work-Related Contexts: A guide to successful Practice* (QCA, 1999).

Stern H H, *Fundamental Concepts of Language Teaching* (Oxford University Press, 1983)

Stevick E., *Evaluating and adapting language materials* (H Allen and R Campbell eds) *Teaching English as a Second Language*: 2nd edn. (New York: McGraw-Hill, 1971: 102–7)

Sutton S, *Assessment: A framework for Teachers, Chapter 2: Managing Assessment.* (NFER, 1991)

Chapter 10

Primary foreign languages: the Key Stage 2–3 transfer point

Ann Gregory

There is considerable overlap between the social milieu of Gardner's socio-educational model and Dörnyei's learner level. Gardner maintains that if the cultural belief is that to learn a foreign language is difficult, then the general level of achievement is likely to be low. The converse also applies. What if the cultural belief is that to learn a foreign language is something which does not start until secondary school? What if an attempt is made to change this perception? Are there also benefits to be gained at Dörnyei's language level? If there are any gains, are these being built upon at secondary school?

Introduction

> *The acquisition of foreign language skills and the development of attitudes towards foreign language learning during later years may be powerfully influenced by the learners' initial experience of success or failure in the language learning situation.*
> (Burstall 1974: 238)

The Early Teaching of Modern Foreign Languages (ETML) re-emerged as an important educational debate in the 1990s, and the recent government initiative to look again at the introduction of foreign languages into the primary curriculum highlights the need to consider prior learning at the start of Key Stage 3, at which point the inclusion of a modern foreign language on the curriculum currently becomes a legal requirement. If positive attitudes towards a subject can be encouraged at an early age, motivation to succeed in the subject increases, and consequently achievement is enhanced. Harley (1986), Singleton (1989), and Johnstone (1994) agree that when children start to learn a foreign language before the age of 11, their attitudes towards continuing to learn the language, towards speakers of that language, the countries where that language is spoken, and indeed learning another foreign language, are more positive than for those children whose first foreign language-learning experience begins in secondary school, or later.

The following findings relating to attitudes towards primary languages are largely the result of post-graduate research, based on a case-study of two village primary schools where French is established as part of the curriculum. The study set out to build a picture of the influences, attitudes and effects of primary foreign language learning, and was based on observations, interviews, pupil-diaries and questionnaires. The pupils were the main focus, although the headteachers, primary teachers, parents and secondary heads of foreign languages departments were also involved. The study covered two years, between 1994 and 1996, and consciously considered the point of transfer from primary to secondary school for a small group of pupils. Inevitably, there were several secondary schools who received the primary pupils, but this study focused on five main receiving schools. It became possible to suggest some of the key factors which affected attitudes and to identify some examples of good practice among the secondary teachers of modern languages. Also highlighted was the obvious need for communication and constructive dialogue between the two Key Stages. This was an area of concern mentioned by Burstall (1974) which is sadly still not resolved in most ETML schemes today.

Focus

The two tables below give a picture of the focus primary schools and their associated secondary schools. The approach to ETML was quite different in each school, reflecting the national picture of *ad hocism* in England, as reported by the 1995 Centre for Language Teaching and Research (CILT) survey. This estimated that among the 5%–7% of state primary school pupils learning a foreign language, there were as many different ways of doing it as there were schools involved. The two target schools reflected some of these differences:

School	Size/Location	Teacher qualification /level	No. of pupils learning French	Timetable allocation	Feeder secondary schools
A	28 pupils 2 classes: Key Stages 1&2 Rural village Victorian building	A level. CAES* in ETML. Support from visiting native French students and ITT (French) students.	14 Key Stage 2	10–15 mins per day plus 30 mins sessions when appropriate. Topic based.	VWXYZ
B	93 pupils 3 classes. Reception-Year 6. New village school replacing several smaller schools.	A level plus. Support from visiting native French students and ITT (French) students.	25 Top Year 4 to Year 6.	Timetabled 40 mins per week. Specialist teaching. Some embedding[1] based on topic.	VWXYZ

*CAES – Certificate in Advanced Educational Studies

How did the two target schools approach ETML? One school had a specialist teacher of French taking 40-minute timetabled classes once a week; the other had an enthusiastic non-specialist, building French into a four-year rolling programme of topics, to allow for the wide age range within each class; she had also started teaching French *on the carpet* for the fifteen minutes each day when the desks were set as lunch tables. In both schools the aims were similar and included:

- building linguistic competence and confidence;
- enjoyment;
- developing positive attitudes;
- increasing cultural and language awareness.

In the receiving secondary schools, there was also a variety of structures and organisational differences, and although the foreign language teaching necessarily conformed to National Curriculum requirements, methods of delivery varied. The catchment areas and pupil achievements differed; two schools were in a city where the eleven-plus exam had been retained.

School	Type	Arrangements for transfer	Organisation of foreign languages	Recognition of prior French?
V	11–18 comprehensive. 900 pupils.	Open day includes French lesson.	All Year 7 French. Top sets in Year 8 French +German.	No.
W	11–16 secondary modern. 400 pupils.	Open day.	Only French taught.	No.
X	11-18 city grammar. 690 pupils.	Open day.	Year 7 French. Setted Year 8. German as option Year 10.	No, except for ex-prep school pupils, who have extension work.
Y	11-16 rural comprehensive. 350 pupils.	Open day.	Year 7 French. German as option Year 9.	No.
Z	11-18 urban C of E comprehensive. 1,300 pupils.	Open day. Over 80 feeder schools.	All Year 7 French. All Year 8 also German.	No, due to unusually large number of feeder schools.

The other points noted about the secondary schools were the differences in:

- timetabled hours for foreign language;
- the numbers of pupils reaching grade C and above in GCSE;
- the resulting sixth form group sizes;
- initiatives involving pupil links and exchanges.

as well as the following differences:

- School W lost many more pupils to the local grammar school and had falling rolls;
- School Z, taking pupils from the whole diocese, found it impossible to set pupils according to their prior experience of learning French;

- School X, ranking highly in the league tables, had 30% of pupils with primary French, but did not consider the implications of this to be a problem;
- in Schools V and Y the heads of languages had taught in the same school for many years.

Pupils, teachers and parents participated in the study:

- in total 108 pupils learning French participated in the two-year project; a group of eleven pupils transferring to three different secondary schools (X,Y and Z) contributed to the more detailed picture of the Key Stage 2/3 transfer;
- 6 primary teachers (including two headteachers, one of whom taught) and five secondary heads of languages;
- 31 parents, who represented a 70% response in school A and 69% in school B.

Factors influencing primary pupil attitudes to French

In this case study, the following factors were identified as influences on pupils' attitudes to learning French:

- **The pupils' perceptions:**
  - their perceptions of level of enjoyment;
  - difficulty of the subject;
  - progress, academic ability;
  - their level of anxiety, embarrassment, self-esteem; personality, gender and age.
- **The teacher:**
  - the classroom environment;
  - European awareness;
  - language awareness;
  - methodology;
  - linguistic confidence and ability;
  - enthusiasm and attitude to the language.
- **The school context:** in the primary school:
  - the links and liaison with other primary schools;

- the support of the headteacher and other staff, the support of parents and governors, the support of the Local Education Authority (LEA) and local Initial Teacher Training (ITT)/In-service (Inset) providers in the secondary school;
- the teacher's attitudes to ETML;
- acknowledgement of prior experience, their expectations, organisation and methods.

- **The subject: French:** pupils reflected on their perceptions of:
  - the usefulness of French, their enjoyment of the subject;
  - the **fun** element, perceived progress, the approach, e.g. embedded or topic-based, the classroom environment, the resources and methods, and the progression to secondary, their attitudes to other languages.
- **Influences outside school:**
  - foreign visits;
  - foreign visitors;
  - media awareness;
  - perceived usefulness for e.g. secondary school, future jobs and travel, and local and national needs.
- **Family and friends:** the attitudes of:
  - parents;
  - siblings and friends;
  - contacts with France, visits abroad and the language experiences of other members of the family.

Comments from the transfer pupils

Though this study was limited to a very small sample, detailed individual pupil profiles covering the eighteen-month period were obtained by means of questionnaire, pupil diaries and discussion with parents. Eleven pupils (two from school A and nine from school B) who transferred to three different secondary schools (X, Y and Z) also reflected on the transfer to a new school and their experience of different teaching and learning styles. Three of these pupils were identified to describe their responses in more detail:

- pupil J who retained positive attitudes to French;

- pupil L who retained negative attitudes;
- pupil T who began to show some negative attitudes after transfer to secondary school.

Pupil J

Pupil J started French in Year 4 at school A, moved to another school for one year before returning to school A for Year 6. He then transferred to School X. His teacher regarded him as very motivated to learn in general and to learn French in particular. He was regarded as '*good at French*'. His family had been abroad; he had a sister who was studying French; he had had contact with a French exchange visitor. His mother had learnt French at school, but had not enjoyed it. Nevertheless, she had found French useful. His mother felt that learning French at primary school would be helpful to him in secondary school. In discussion, however, she said that more important than French was learning the basics of English grammar. In the second questionnaire, completed when pupil J had been at secondary school for a year, his mother suggested that French should be taught to all primary pupils, possibly from the age of seven. She acknowledged that, '*knowing some of the basics to start with gave him an advantage at secondary school*', and that her son clearly enjoyed French.

Pupil J's initial diary entry in Year 6 summed up his feelings about primary French:

> *I find French particularly difficult because I did French one year and then missed a year and started French again. I find counting easier than actual words. Learning French now will give you a head start when you reach secondary school. I enjoy doing French even though I find it difficult.*

One of the lesson evaluation sheets showed his reaction to a particular lesson:

> *I liked it because it was interesting.*
>
> *I have enjoyed the French we have done, especially eating the French food.*
>
> *It is difficult but I enjoy it. I worked well and had a good try.*

He was aware of his progress:

> *I feel I understood some of the pictures and yesterday was the first time I had done the parts of the body and now I am quite confident about them.*

However, there was a lot still to learn: his Eiffel Tower colouring to show his progress was only filled in to the base of the pillar by the end of Year 6 (see

Appendix p129 for sample Eiffel Tower). He showed that he was implementing learning strategies to facilitate his retention of vocabulary:

> *To try and make French words easier to learn. If I can I compare it with an English word.*

He recognised the support the teacher gave through gestures:

> *It also makes it easier if the teacher gives actions or points.*

He commented on a session which had been organised as a carousel of activities supervised by a number of student teachers:

> *I especially liked making Maurice (a moving puppet). I found making Maurice the easiest because I had done the parts of the body on the computer just before. I found the dancing the hardest. The people who did the dancing spoke the most French. It was really difficult. The people who did the cooking spoke quite a lot of French, but gave actions so you knew what they were doing. I liked it on the computer because the people who were doing it with us had to think about the different parts, so that gave me a little more confidence. All in all I enjoyed yesterday afternoon.*

On transfer to secondary school, pupil J continued to enjoy French. He wrote: '*I still enjoy French just as much as before*'. He was convinced that primary French had been helpful to him and had given him confidence. He recognised a difference in the teaching/learning experience: '*I learn French completely differently*'. Writing was a novelty: '*We never wrote any French down at my old school*'. On the reverse of the questionnaire sheet he wrote a 'basic conversation': '*Bonjour. Je m'appelle (name). Je ai 11 ans. Je habite Ripon en Angleterre*' *(sic)*. On the questionnaire he confirmed: '*I think that doing primary French will help me in secondary school*' and added '*IT HAS DONE*'. He did, however, regret not having done any writing at primary school and thought that all primary pupils should learn some French, '*then all the class would be at about the same level of understanding*'.

Pupil L

Pupil L transferred to school B after his parents separated. He started French in Year 6 and then transferred to school X. His mother had learnt French and had found it both enjoyable and useful. Assessed by his teacher as lacking motivation for learning generally and for learning French in particular, he was nonetheless regarded as a very capable pupil in French in Year 6. He said that he disliked French more than other subjects. This disenchantment was out of line with the attitudes of his peers, and perhaps reflected more a personal anxiety than an entirely subject-specific problem.

After two lessons of French in Year 6 he wrote in his diary:

> *When I first had a French lesson I was worried and felt left out. I like my French name, Albert, but I don't understand much at all, being new. It's very hard to understand what the teacher is on about. I only enjoy it a bit but not very much.*

The following term he ticked the 'unhappy' face on a lesson evaluation and said that he had only learnt the French name for stick insect. When a group of French teacher training students were in school and teaching a little French every day, he said, '*with French daily it is boring because you have it too often*'. However, he felt that he worked '*average* or *medium*' *(sic)* and showed his progress on the Eiffel Tower scale as above the second platform, although he had previously ticked the statement '*I'm no good at French*'. He recorded an interest in learning about French traditions and customs, but said that he would not like to visit France. He disliked the French teacher and the way French was taught, but did recognise that it might help him in secondary school. He was able to identify the exact date when he had started to learn French, thus emphasising the impact of this day on his life.

Pupil L's dislike of French continued into his first year at secondary school, as reflected in the consistency in his responses in the questionnaire. He was aware that his parents supported primary French and that it had been useful to him in secondary school. He commented on the increased pace in lessons, with little time for recap and revision, compared to a more relaxed teaching style in primary school: '*We get much faster here at (school X) rather than more gradual learning as at (school B)*'. He remembered primary activities as '*more enjoyable*'. Interestingly, pupil L's mother stated on her questionnaire that her children were *very keen*. There was evidently a mismatch with her son's perceptions here. However, on the second parental questionnaire, the comment was made: '*He doesn't like it as much – more serious now*'. The secondary approach was seen as '*less fun*'.

Pupil T

Pupil T started French in school B and transferred to school Y for Year 7. He was assessed by his primary teacher as being well motivated to learn and highly motivated to learn French, a subject in which he appeared very able. His mother and sister spoke a little French but his father none at all. The family had visited France twice, and pupil T had attended a private French Club. He learned French for a total of three years at primary school and found it '*enjoyable, fun, interesting* and *useful*'. In one diary entry he wrote:

> *When I first started French, I remember I felt excited and wondering if I can remember all the French words. I think that our school has become quite famous for doing French, mainly because we have been in the paper a couple of times.*

Later he reflected:

> *French was at first a bit boring to me but now I'm finding it more interesting because we're doing things that are funny. To have fun in a lesson is very important because you remember.*

Pupil T's class had a French national student working with them for eight weeks and he wrote: *I like Sylvie*, although he later decided that to have **three** French students for **three** weeks was too much French:

> *The worst bit was when the French students Sylvie, Sophie and Valerie came. I didn't like it very much because every day for the three weeks they were here we did French every day so that it got a bit boring.*

His favourite 'French experience' was '*when we got to try the croissans and french bread with chocholate drink*' (sic). On an individual lesson evaluation, he assessed his progress by confidently filling in the Eiffel Tower to the second platform level. He wrote: '*I feel that French is very educational and should be compulsory*'. He acknowledged, however, that it was not too difficult: '*I worked in between hard and layed back*' *(sic)*. Pupil T said that he would like to learn other languages and that French had helped him. His positive attitude to French was recognised by his mother, who appreciated the relaxed approach and *fun* methods, compared to the grammatical approach she had experienced. She said she had found her languages useful, but had not enjoyed learning them at school.

After transfer to school Y, pupil T began to be less positive in his attitudes. By the end of Year 7 he recorded for the first time on his questionnaire that he didn't like French, that it was hard and boring, that he didn't like the French teacher, nor the way in which they were being taught French, and that he wouldn't like to go to France.The main barrier to his enjoyment seemed to be the teacher:

> *I liked French in the primary school a lot better than here at seniors. I think that the French teacher is not strict enough but because he lets us mess about we never get any work done and we don't learn.*

The three years' primary French and the pupil's level of achievement had not been recognised in Year 7. Pupil T's mother, in her second questionnaire, also noted that his enjoyment had lessened: '*He doesn't enjoy it as much. He feels it was more fun to learn at primary school*'. She noticed more emphasis on writing skills, with poor reinforcement of good pronunciation and communication.

Discussion

These individual responses from pupils and their parents serve to illustrate the complexity of the task of identifying specific issues, factors and incidents which affect attitudes to primary foreign languages. Rather than one individual factor, several factors working together can be seen to influence attitudes. For example, in the case of pupil J, factors such as self-esteem and self-confidence in a relaxed and supportive atmosphere, alongside attractive teaching methods and a good relationship with the teacher, contribute to positive attitudes, despite a lack of strong parental support for primary languages. In the case of pupil L, the effect of family circumstances, a lack of general motivation for school work, a feeling of isolation and inferiority compared to his peers, and a dislike of oral activities all contributed towards initial negative attitudes which, once established, were sustained in the secondary phase. For pupil T it appears that the teacher, the change of teaching styles and methods and a failure to recognise prior knowledge in the secondary school were the main contributory factors in his change of attitude. In all of these cases, the teacher and the teacher's personality were central.

Conclusion

Thus even in a very small sample, this case study has raised some of the issues which surround the transfer between Key Stages 2 and 3 in relation to attitudes to foreign language learning. Sadly, many of the tensions and anxieties uncovered in the Burstall report (Burstall, 1974) still exist, and it is only by improving opportunities for dialogue between the two phases that a cohesive language plan can be created, where the largely positive attitudes engendered in the primary school can continue to flourish through to the secondary, and where each individual pupil's needs can be recognised and met. This is the challenge for the millennium.

Ann Gregory's case studies suggest that social milieu influenced by encouragement from parents for the learning of foreign languages, and the appreciation of secondary schools that foreign languages teaching and learning has taken place in some primary schools, can have a positive effect on pupils' motivation. Gardner also identifies the role of

- self-esteem;
- a stress-free learning environment;
- teaching methods;
- rapport with the teacher;
- group cohesion.

Catering for both those with and those without foreign language learning experience in the primary school presents a considerable challenge in terms of differentiation. It is a challenge which has to be taken on, however, if pupils' motivation for learning foreign languages is to be maintained and, preferably, enhanced at the KS2/KS3 transfer point. If Ann Gregory's findings, on the basis of this small sample, are generalisable, it appears that the challenge is often being ignored. It is hoped that this may change, indeed it must, especially at a time when support for foreign language teaching at KS 2 is being provided by the National Curriculum, even if not in the form of a statutory requirement.

Bibliograhy

Burstall C, *Primary French in the Balance* (NFER, 1974)

Centre for Information on Language Teaching and Research. *Survey of Modern Foreign Languages in the Primary School* (CILT, 1995)

Gregory A J *Primary Foreign Language Teaching-Influences, Attitudes and Effects.* Unpublished thesis for M.Ed. (University of Leeds, 1996)

Harley B, *Age in Second Language Acquisition* (Multilingual Matters, 1986)

Johnstone R, *Teaching Foreign Languages in the Primary School. Approaches and Implications.* (Scottish Council for Educational Research, 1994)

Singleton D, *Language Acquisition: The Age Factor* (Multilingual Matters, 1989)

Notes

1 i.e. linking the foreign language to other areas of the curriculum and using it as a natural means of communication in the classroom, e.g. checking dinner numbers, celebrating birthdays, revising maths tables.

Appendix

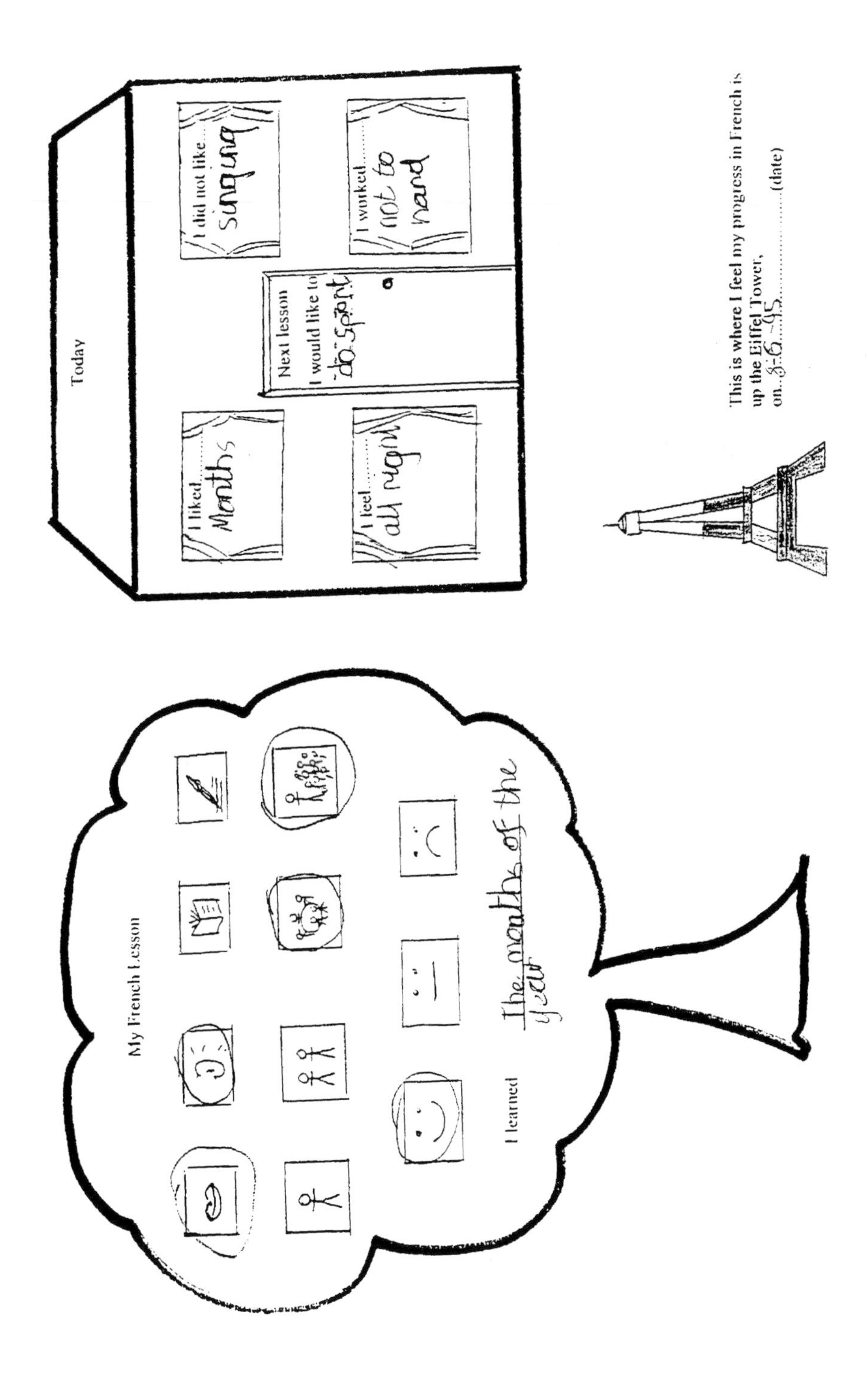
Today
I liked... Months
I did not like... singing
Next lesson I would like to do sport
I feel... all right
I worked... not to hard
This is where I feel my progress in French is up the Eiffel Tower, on 8-6-95 (date)
My French Lesson
I learned The months of the year

Chapter 11

Where do we go from here?

Gary Chambers

As teachers, we appreciate the opportunity to share ideas and exchange strategies which have been successful. Implementing other colleagues' ideas is not always problem-free, however. They may have worked for them and their pupils in their particular context, but a successful transfer to another context is not guaranteed. This is where consideration of why the strategy worked is so important and sound theoretical underpinning such as that provided by Dörnyei and Gardner are crucial. These help us create a template which allows successful transfer to take place.

The contributors to this book have provided suggestions which can make the teaching and learning experience better. What more can and perhaps should be done on a macro level to enhance learners' motivation? Society, government, school management teams all have a role to play to combat a situation in which, according to one of the main findings of the Nuffield Report (Nuffield Languages Foundation, 2000: 7):

> *... current provision does not motivate and too many pupils, also lacking positive messages about languages from outside the classroom, see language learning as irrelevant.*

What follows are some recommendations which may make a contribution to this macro view of motivation and foreign language learning. It is acknowledged that some may appear idealistic. Some are fraught with difficulty. If we are serious about education, however, and the place of foreign language learning in education, then surely a little idealism is not misplaced.

The status of modern foreign languages

Major policy decisions have to be made to enhance the status of foreign languages in schools:

- The proposal that we should 'invest in an early start' (Nuffield Languages Foundation, 2000: 89) and teach foreign languages at KS2 (QCA/DfEE, 1999: 11) should be implemented with appropriate resources allocated to the training of primary school teachers; equally important is the recognition of pupils' learning in the primary school by teachers of languages at KS3.
- Rather than a second foreign language (and maybe even the first foreign language) being squeezed out of a packed National Curriculum, it should be given its proper place on the school timetable as is the case in most other European countries. Claude Allègre, French Education Minister, announced in July 1998 (*Times Educational Supplement*, 10.7.98, p.25) the requirement for *Lycéens* to have competence in at least two foreign languages by the time they leave school. By contrast David Blunkett, British Secretary of State for Education and Employment, announced in the same month (*Times Educational Supplement* 10.7.98, p.21) that some pupils should be allowed to drop a modern foreign language in Key Stage 4. (See also DfEE, 1998b.)
- A foreign language should be compulsory until pupils leave school. Arguably, it should be a university entrance requirement; this is a view supported by Clark (1995: 21):

  > *What is needed is a radical linguistic policy and huge investment: two foreign languages for all children starting one at age seven, the other at age nine, with a choice of vocational or academic streams from 12 for pupils with different career inclinations. By 2005 there should be no entry to university without two foreign languages.*

The Nuffield Report (Nuffield Languages Foundation, 2000:7) calls for languages to be 'a requirement for entry to higher education and for designated vocational qualifications'. It has to be acknowledged, however, that such a requirement could backfire for modern languages, by making it the most hated subject area on the curriculum. The situation is far from simple.

If reforms such as those suggested above were to be implemented, then future generations of pupils would be more likely to see for themselves the importance of foreign languages. They would receive greater encouragement from parents, who would not only share this perception of the importance of foreign language competence but also be able to offer practical support to their children because of their own competence.

- The range and balance of languages offered in school needs to be addressed (Nuffield Languages Foundation, 2000: 90). The programme of diversification of first foreign languages should be revived to enhance the importance of foreign language learning generally, as opposed to the 'traditional' focus on French. Diversification is a term now rarely used in the context of foreign language learning and teaching and appears to have been crushed beneath the landslide of other reforms, league tables and OFSTED inspections, as well as teacher supply. Languages, not just French, and how they are learned, have to be seen as having an important role to play in the lives of our young people in the 21st century.

The European Dimension

There is a need for the EC resolution of 24th May 1988 and the subsequent Department for Education (DFE) policy statement (February 1991), requiring the inclusion of a European Dimension in the National Curriculum, to be implemented with enthusiasm and energy, at least at KS1 and KS2. There are examples of good practice throughout the country, but they tend to be the exception rather than the rule and to focus on French. Pupils must be given insight into a wider range of languages, people and cultures if problems of ignorance and ill-founded prejudice are to be obviated.

The cultural dimension

Culture should be given its proper place in the foreground of the language learning experience, to emphasise how culture and language are inextricably linked. This may enhance the level of interest of pupils and others at every stage of the language learning process and may serve to prevent stereotyping and the consolidation of prejudice based on ignorance. If pupils cannot go to the country, then the country should come to them in the form of visits from foreign nationals who live and work locally, visits to local businesses who communicate and trade with our EU partners, the organisation of German/French/Spanish days inside and outside school. If motivation is to be high, then the foreign language must be kept at the top of the agenda, as a subject of practical and vocational application and intrinsic interest, as opposed to just another academic subject on the school timetable.

The teacher

Teachers have a key role to play in motivation. They are more important than the methodology, working environment or equipment. Their support, enthusiasm, positive approach in providing a learning experience which has practical application, vocational value and is enjoyable and fulfilling are key motivational components. It is important that teachers access their pupils' views on their learning experience in order to provide for their varying needs. If these needs are to be met, teachers must be provided with the necessary in-service training (for example in ICT and autonomous/flexible approaches to learning), the necessary resources (for example computer hard- and software and adequate teaching space, preferably in the form of smaller classes), time (to properly plan and prepare lessons), support (classroom assistants and, in the increasingly technological world of modern language teaching and learning, technicians) and a syllabus which takes them away from purely transactional language into greater linguistic variety.

The timetable

Lee and Dickson (1991: 10) identify the length and frequency of lessons as an area of particular concern to UK teachers of modern languages:

> *The teachers stressed the need for languages to be taught in short periods (one suggested no more than 30-minute sessions), with frequent lessons during the week: the 'little and often' approach.*

A timetable which seems in most schools to be driven by science and technology departments is unlikely to provide much scope for single lessons. An allocation of one or two teaching periods per week of 70 minutes duration for foreign languages appears to be the norm. This falls some way short of meeting the needs of learners, especially the disaffected (Chambers, 1992) for whom a 'little but often' approach is almost certainly more appropriate.

Conclusion

Motivation is the key which unlocks the door to the solutions to most foreign-language-teaching-and-learning-specific concerns. It is the foundation upon which we succeed or fail and upon which our pupils succeed or fail. It shows the way to good teaching and learning which help league tables, OFSTED inspections and other related issues look after themselves. The contributors to this book have described how they have tackled the motivation issue and justified why they did it their way. Maybe they have helped you to look at your successes and review why they worked. Do not be tempted to minimise or trivialise their importance. They are worth sharing with colleagues. Each success represents an important contribution to the enhancement of pupils' motivation, their learning experience and achievement.

Bibliography

Chambers G, 'Modern languages and the timetable' in *Language Learning Journal*, 5: 55–59 (1992)

Clark R, 'A tongue-tied time warp' in *Times Higher Educational Supplement,* 13th October, p.21 (1995)

DFE *The European Dimension in Education* (HMSO/DFE, 1991)

DfEE, The Education (National Curriculum) (Exceptions at Key Stage 4) Regulations 1998 (Statutory Instruments 1998 No 2021) (DfEE, 1998b)

Lee B and P Dickson, *Foreign Languages for Lower Attaining Pupils* (NFER, 1991)

The Nuffield Languages Inquiry, *Languages: the next generation: a summary of the final report of the Nuffield Languages Inquiry* (The Nuffield Foundation, 2000a)

QCA/DfEE, The review of the national curriculum in England. The Secretary of State's proposals, (QCA, 1999)

The contributors

Jenifer Alison has worked in primary and secondary schools and is currently PGCE tutor for Modern Languages at St Martin's College, Lancaster. Her main interest is in finding ways to motivate and help pupils with learning difficulties access the National Curriculum. Using a vocational approach with disaffected learners in Year 9 and Key Stage 4 has been the main focus of her research, a large part of which has involved regular teaching in local schools of classes with a sizeable proportion of pupils with emotional and behavioural difficulties. She is the author of practical books and articles on the subject and has produced a Certificate of Achievement in Modern Language Skills for Work.

Amanda Barton is Lecturer in Education at the University of Manchester where she is the Subject Leader for the Modern Foreign Languages PGCE course.

Prior to taking up her appointment at Manchester in September 1999, she was employed at the Language Centre, University of Warwick, to teach German on a range of courses to undergraduates, postgraduates, business people, GCSE pupils and A level students. During this time she also worked as a supply teacher in schools in Coventry and Warwickshire, and as the Editorial Administrator for a feminist academic journal, *Gender and Education*. Before moving to Warwick, she worked as a teacher of German, French and English in a 13–18 school in Staffordshire.

Her doctoral research investigated pupils' responses to modern foreign language learning in the context of national concern about boys' performance and focused specifically on the effects of single-sex grouping.

Kim Brown has been involved in language teaching for over twenty years. She moved from teaching French in secondary schools to initial teacher training, firstly in the Language Teaching Centre at the University of York and, for the last five years, at the University of East Anglia. Her particular interests are in cross-curricular approaches to modern language learning, a subject on which she has written books and chapters in books. She is currently conducting a longitudinal study on the experiences and careers of language teachers in their first five years of teaching.

Mike Calvert is a Lecturer in the School of Education, University of Sheffield. He began his career as a teacher of Spanish and French and went on to work at the University of York where he produced Spanish teaching materials for publication and where he was responsible for an action research programme for teachers of modern languages. He currently works in the area of initial teacher education and is responsible for the MEd distance learning courses in Educational Management.

Jane Cavani is Lecturer in Modern Languages at the University of Glasgow's Crichton Campus in Dumfries. She has held posts as a lectrice teaching English at the Université de Caen in Normandy, a lecturer in French language, literature and civilisation within the French Department of the University of Glasgow and a Research Fellow for Scottish CILT based at the University of Stirling. She has published within the academic field of French literature and politics in both Britain and France, but more recently has co-authored research studies into language learning in Scottish schools for both Glasgow City Council and the Scottish Office Education and Industry Department (now the Scottish Executive Education Department).

Gary Chambers taught German and Latin in secondary schools in Cleveland and London before joining the School of Education, University of Leeds, in 1989. He plays a major role in the pre- and in-service training of modern languages teachers and is also Head of Undergraduate Studies in Education. His major research interest is motivation and foreign language learning. He has co-directed projects on teaching foreign languages to pupils with special educational needs, diversification and 'bilingual' teaching of geography and history.

Susan Chamberlain is Principal Teacher of Modern Languages at Viewforth High School in Kirkaldy, Fife. As a teacher for 25 years and a mother of three, she thinks she has seen and heard it all before and then discovers she has not. As long as the element of surprise continues, so will she.

Steven Fawkes is Education Officer and Development Officer at the BBC, working within the Factual and Learning directorate. The focus of his work at the BBC has been on television and radio programmes for language learners in schools, and has broadened to include published and interactive resources and website development. Previously Steven taught French and German in Durham and was Curriculum Support Teacher for Languages in County Durham, working in INSET and Curriculum Development in classrooms in comprehensive and special schools throughout the county. Steven is an author of resources for teachers and pupils and contributes to academic and professional journals. He is a regular contributor to conferences across the UK. In 2000–2001 Steven is President of the Association for Language Learning.

Ann Gregory taught French to secondary school pupils in Yorkshire and to middle school pupils in Northumberland before joining the staff at the College of Ripon and York Saint John in 1990. She is responsible for MFL and methodology support within the undergraduate primary teacher training programme and in-service courses, and has worked on Lingua projects relating to early language learning. She acts as MFL Consultant to the City of York LEA and is involved in the DfEE primary languages initiative. Her recent MEd focused on the influences, attitudes and effects of early language learning.

Terry Lamb works in the School of Education at the University of Nottingham, having previously taught German and French in schools in London and Derbyshire. He is Director of the European PGCE programme as well as Course Director of the MA in Urban Education and Social Policy. A member of the Centre for Research into Second and Foreign Language Pedagogy, he carries out research and supervises research students in the areas of learner autonomy, motivation, languages policy and community languages, fields in which he has published widely. He is an EU expert in Intercultural Education, an active member of several European research networks, and has carried out consultancy work for the Ministries of Education in the Czech Republic and Malaysia, as well as in the UK.

Keith Marshall has been a lecturer in French at University of Wales, Bangor since 1970. From 1990–94 he directed the Enterprise in Higher Education Programme at Bangor. In 1994 he set up Bangor outposts of CILT's Comenius network and the European Commission's network of European Resources Centres for schools. He lectures on 18th century French literature and coordinates the University's Languages for Non-Specialists programme. Besides some work on motivation in language learning, he is currently compiling, for the University Council of Modern Languages, statistics on the numbers involved in UK language learning from GCSE to PhD.

Jim McElwee works for the advisory service of Redcar and Cleveland LEA and is also ICT Project Officer in the East Cleveland Education Action Zone. He taught modern languages for twenty years and has been interested in ICT in the teaching and learning of MFL since 1984. Much of his work has been with pupils with low prior attainment and poor motivation. He has been involved in the production of CD-ROMs in French, Spanish and German, and other computer-based materials. He is currently researching the potential of ICT for teaching languages in primary schools.

David Stork started teaching in Co. Durham, becoming Head of Modern Languages in an 11–18 comprehensive in the East Riding in 1980. He was appointed Senior Teacher (curriculum and timetable) in 1988. From 1996 he served as Link Adviser with a general brief on the creation of East Riding Unitary Authority. He is also responsible for MFL, International dimension and Post-16, including Key Skills and oversight of GNVQ. David is Co-ordinator of the Yorkshire Rose Comenius Centre.